T0104208

IT'S *OKAY*
NOT TO LOOK FOR
THE MEANING
OF LIFE

IT'S OKAY
NOT TO LOOK FOR
THE MEANING
OF LIFE

**A Zen Monk's Guide to Living
Stress-Free One Day at a Time**

Jikisai Minami

TUTTLE Publishing

Tokyo │ Rutland, Vermont │ Singapore

Contents

CHAPTER ONE
What Is the "Self" You Value?

Live Life to the Full While Looking Death in the Face

A Technique for Living

After spending nearly twenty years as a monk at Eiheiji Temple in Fukui Prefecture, by chance I became the acting chief priest of Osorezan, a Buddhist temple on the sacred Mount Osore in Aomori Prefecture, more than ten years ago.

This may shock you, but I did not become a monk because I had noble aspirations to help others. Ever since I can remember, I have had unresolved issues within me and the only way I have been able to deal with them during my life on this earth is to become ordained. That is the honest truth. I have been attracted to Buddhism since I encountered the Buddha's words, "All actions are impermanent," when I was in the third grade of junior high school; so after two years of working in an office after graduating from college, I chose to become a monk.

Since then, I have been working on my own problems, but as I continued my training and began to have my voice heard in various places, I realized for the first time that there are many people who experience the same difficulties in life as I do. These people may seem happy in the eyes of others, but they are not experiencing fulfillment. They are not going through any particular difficulties, but life is somehow suffocating. They can't get rid of a feeling of unease in their everyday lives. These are the people I am talking about.

If you have a problem, you can be sure that others have

that problem too. Whenever possible, I have started to meet and talk with those who contact me, to discuss their needs. I have never counted how many people I have met, but it has been about twenty years since I started such dialogues. As I listen to the stories of those who say they are suffering, I notice something.

If you look at a problem clearly, you will often find that the solution is closer to home than you think. It also means that if you know who "you" really are, you can lessen the pain and live a little more easily. In this book, I will share what I have felt in my conversations with the people I have met and what I have been thinking about as a monk on a daily basis. This is not a book about Buddhism itself. Please think of it as a book that uses the tools of Buddhism to learn about the true nature of suffering caused by obsessions and attachments, and how to handle that suffering.

I have not given "answers" to the people I have met so far. I only hope that their problems have been mirrored and clarified in the course of our conversation. That's all I've been thinking as I talked to them.

I hope that as you read through this book, it will help you see your situation in a completely different light. That will be enough for me. Once the true identity of what is tormenting or troubling you is revealed, you will see that there is surely a way out of it. When you can see the way forward, you can take a step out of any predicament.

If there is a heavy feeling inside you right now, it's difficult to simply wish it away. You know you shouldn't have this feeling, but the fact that you keep holding on to it is because it's not something that can be thrown away in the first place. But even if we can't eliminate suffering, we can relieve worries and problems. More to the point, it is possible to live a life that is "okay"—even if it's hard.

Of course, there is nothing better than to be able to live happily every day. In fact, there are many people who enjoy their lives without much difficulty and without recourse to Buddhism. I think that's fine: in fact, I would prefer that all people lived like that, and for Buddhism to cease to exist.

However, if you feel that you want to change your current situation, it is not a bad idea to try the tools of Buddhism.

Buddhism declares that life is hard, painful, sad and miserable. Even so, we live with everything we have until we die. That courage is what is precious. To live a life in which one can say, "I'm glad to be alive, despite everything"; to leave this world saying, "Living wasn't so bad after all."

Buddhism is a technique for living. Actually, to be precise, it is a technique for living while facing death. In this book, I will hand over one of the tools of Buddhism to you. It is a tool, so you won't know if it is useful or not until you use it yourself. I hope you will try it first to see if it really works for you. After all, a good pair of scissors for me may not be easy for someone else to use. But I will be happy if this tool is of some use to you as you navigate your daily life.

—Jikisai Minami

Chapter One

What Is the "Self" You Value?

Stop taking care of yourself

People are born into this world by chance.

There is a way of life in which we can
come to terms with ourselves.

Instead of confronting suffering, we can
adjust to painful situations and work our
way through them.

When I talk with people who come to me for life counseling, I find that most of them have a particular misconception. That is, they believe that there is a presence called the "self," and that they must take care of that self. So, they are frustrated with their daily lives, and with relationships that are not going the way they want them to, thinking that their precious self needs to have a fuller life. They are impatient, thinking surely their lives can be better. There are many people who think this.

You may think it's natural for you to have a "self" and for you to take care of that self. But what is the self? Is it the body? Not really. Each cell in the body is replaced every three months, making the body itself into a new entity.

As to whether the heart is the self, again, this is not provable. If you were asked how you could prove that the "heart of yesterday" is the same as the "heart of today," you would be at a loss for an answer. To begin with, there are only two grounds on which we can say that "yesterday's self" and "today's self" are the same. The first is one's own memory and the second is "recognition from others"—that's it.

For example, what would happen if you woke up tomorrow morning and all the memories of everything you've ever done were gone? The "I" you are thinking of now would no longer exist. Or, what would you do if tomorrow everyone around you said you were a different person called X? Your choices would then be either to live as X, to suffer from mental illness or to commit suicide. I am not exaggerating. That is how fragile the "self" is.

The basis of the self is twofold: first the consciousness that I am "me," and then to be recognized as "me" by others. If either or both of these are lost, the basis for being oneself disappears, and the "I" or "me" collapses on the spot. What you usually call "I" or "me" is nothing more than an entity made up of memories and relationships with others. I wonder what we hope to gain by valuing that uncertain "I" that exists on such shaky ground.

When I discuss the concept of "self" with others, they often say, "But I'm here!" or "What is this 'self'?" and they start talking about their name, gender, age, personality, occupation, family, address and so on. But this is just a list of attributes that a person has at a given time.

If you take all those things away, what is left? Human existence is like this: from the moment we are all born, we all continue to wear what we can call the "clothes that others put on us." You did not choose the day, place, gender or physical characteristics of your birth. Even your name was chosen by your parents. Even your parents just happen to be your parents by chance. We are not born with a desire to be born into this world in the first place. Theoretically, if you were born the way you wanted to be, you would be able to decide the day, place and parents of your birth as you wished, and you would most likely be the way you want to be.

But who can say, "I am everything I want to be"?

We are all born into this world by chance and made to be "ourselves" by other people. In order to accept this "self," one must be recognized and praised by others. Since you are wearing clothes chosen by others, not by you, you can only feel relieved and motivated when someone tells you that those clothes look good on you and that they like them.

The greatest human need is to be approved by others—the ones who made us who we are.

In this book I will talk about a way of life in which we can come to terms with the fact that we have been forced to become "ourselves," and, how, instead of confronting any suffering we experience, we can adjust to it and live through it.

It's okay not to look for
the meaning of life

You don't have to strive to lead "a
meaningful life" or "a life worth living."
People can live happily enough without
searching for the meaning of life.

You might think I'm a pretty argumentative monk. But for me, the question, "What am I?" has always positioned itself right at the center of my heart. How did it happen that I came to thinking about the existence of the "self" in this way?

Perhaps the most significant factor was my childhood asthma, which had me going in and out of the hospital from an early age. When a severe seizure strikes, you are close to a state of suffocation and your eyes turn bright red. When this happened to me, I wondered many times in my childish mind whether I was about to die. I still vividly remember the fear and sensation of not knowing what was going to happen. Having these attacks regularly from the age of about three, when my self-awareness had not yet solidified, "death" was far more real to me than "life."

Even when I started to go to school, I was often absent and was behind other students in everything. I was a child who naturally became distant from my surroundings and looked at my friends and teachers with cold eyes. I did not have any solid sense of who I was or what it meant to be alive. "Why do I have to live?" "What am I?" Even as a child, these were compelling questions for me.

During those childhood years, I had an experience that determined the feelings of anxiety I had about life. It happened one evening in my early elementary school years, the day before my weekly hospital visit. When I got home from school that day I thought, "Tomorrow is the hospital," and then I suddenly wondered why my mother was taking me to the hospital. What if she said she wouldn't take me? I wouldn't be able to go by myself, and then I'd be in trouble. And my next thought was "Why is she my parent? What if she says, 'I'm done being your parent'?"

When you start thinking like that, it doesn't stop.

In truth, perhaps everything in the world is simply based on promises, and no one realizes it, so they just carry on living without a care in the world. But when I realized this, I felt an unspeakable sense of dread. It was so terrifying that I felt as if the world I had been living in had been suddenly turned upside down. Ever since then, this fear has occupied my heart and given me a deep-seated insecurity about life. This feeling did not go away when I reached adolescence. Now that I think about it, I was in a very desperate situation back then. Why are we alive? What is the meaning of the self? I read books at random, pondered, and inquired of people I thought would have the answers. But no adult, no book, could give me a satisfactory answer.

In the third year of junior high school, I came across a sentence in the epic fourteenth century literary saga *The Tale of the Heike*, which reads, "All worldly things are impermanent." Generally speaking, this phrase is interpreted to mean that all things in this world change. However, the meaning I perceived was different. Life itself has no meaning. There is no solid basis for my existence. There is no firm basis for human existence. These words left by the Buddha 2,500 years ago taught me that.

At this point, I thought, "I'm saved!" Because I felt that at least there was someone who was suffering the same pain as I was.

Buddha taught me that people are born without their own will and have to live a life for which they have no basis. One has to live with that sense of unwillingness and sadness.

You may think that there is no hope in the words "life is meaningless." But once you know that, you don't have to strive to live a meaningful or worthwhile life. You don't have to be so eager to find life's meaning. Realistically, we can all live without such a thing. In fact, people are living splendidly even if they don't know the meaning of life. One can't help but think about what it all means, though. Others may try to share their own life lessons, but perhaps what they say doesn't add up for you. If a person realizes that there are other ways of seeing the world than just their current point of view, their outlook will change dramatically. Buddhism can provide this new perspective.

In Buddhism there is a saying, "All is pain." Everything in this world is "suffering." Buddha saw this. In fact, there are more sad and painful things in this world than happy and joyful things. So it is no wonder that life is hard and that living is uncomfortable. You might think that we should not be so cynical and should live more joyfully. But seeing things from this point of view can be an intense relief for some people. Which people? The people who have always felt that "life is a struggle," or "I am not a good person to begin with."

These are the people who can't get on board with the "dreams will come true if you work hard" narrative, the ones who are fed up with their own inadequacies. They can't ignore their own difficulties in life. When such people come into contact with Buddhism, they can be relieved to realize that their existence is nothing more than a "borrowed thing" and that they "just happened to be born," as if it was something that they'd always known deep down.

Accepting this borrowed self, somehow cheering it up, encouraging it to be okay and to traverse this world until the day life ends—I think that is one way to live.

Relationships with others are the source of many worries

If you only act on your own assumptions, you may find it difficult to have well-adjusted relationships with others.

Separating "feelings" from "what is currently happening" can bring a problem one step closer to resolution.

There are two types of people who come to me for advice. They are people who are struggling with a complicated situation right now and people who want to get somewhere from the place they are now. What both have in common is that their own story is not the first thing that comes up.

"My child is a social recluse and I don't know what to do."

"I've worked at that place for years, but my boss is too dictatorial and I can't take it anymore."

"I live with my elderly mother and I can't stand the constant abuse from her."

"I want to divorce my husband because I don't love him anymore, but he won't agree and I am in pain."

Of course, the person in question thinks they are talking about their own problem. Most problems, however, no matter how serious and painful, are about the relationships that surround a person: with parents, children, spouse or colleagues.

People who have been suffering a lot with problems in their relationships sometimes come from far away to talk to me—a person they have never met before—about what is on their mind, and while I listen to them, I am aware of the pain they have been going through.

23

But, in these situations, I do not really care how much pain that person is in.

What I listen to carefully is the composition of the relationships behind the emotions. What is the person's relationship to this other person or people, and where is the difficulty? Because only when we see the cast of characters, can we understand the nature of the problem and understand the root of the feelings that are being expressed now.

One day, a single man in his forties came to me for advice. His mother, who he lived with, never stopped commenting on the way he choses to lead his life. She was so domineering that it was hard for him to be around her. What should he do? That was what he was seeking advice about. He had a decent job and was financially stable. A third party could easily see that distancing himself from his mother would solve the problem.

My advice was quite simple. "If you are in so much pain, why don't you just move away for now? Why don't you leave your mother's house and rent an apartment?"

He looked at me with an astonished expression. "You say that, but my mother would just come over to my new place!"

I suggested that if she came over, he could let her stay for a while, then ask her to leave. Then, when she had gone, he could secure his own time and space.

"Right . . . ," he replied. He didn't seem convinced. Although he had earnestly stated that he was in pain, I realized that he really did not want to leave his mother. Of course his mother's presence was annoying to him. But since she cooked all his meals and took care of him, he could enjoy an easy life if he was able put up with a little interference. Would he choose "a convenient life" or "parental over-involvement?" The essence of the problem was simple. But he saw it as something big that he was unable to handle, and he was suffering. My guess was that he had some problems at work or in other relationships, and was taking his depression out on his mother.

When considering interpersonal relationships, it is important to understand that talking about things that are hard or things that you hate is not the same as what is really happening right now. Without first understanding the distinction between those two things, the conversation cannot begin. If people are unable to make this distinction, they will keep going around in circles. If you act on your own assumptions without an accurate understanding of your relationship with the other party, there is no way things will work well. For some people, it's hard to make the distinction between their own feelings and what is actually happening. But if the current situation is not the same as the desired situation, then we must try to look at the problem with clarity. To accomplish this, you have to separate the emotion from the situation.

In short, you have to think calmly. For example, if you say "I don't like my boss and have a hard time going to work," is it a personality clash or is it a bad fit in terms of the job itself? If the former is the case, minimizing the amount of time you spend with your boss outside of work-related needs and learning to use appropriate praise or flattery techniques should improve the situation considerably. If it's the latter, you can try to focus on the task at hand, taking the other party into consideration as a "condition" of the job. If you are prepared to let the other party take credit for a job done well, I think it will be easier to turn things around. If the relationship has deteriorated to the level of workplace bullying, that's a different story. Coping with bullying at work is not something that can be managed by personal techniques alone. But if the issue is at the level of whether you "like" or "dislike" a person or situation, there are steps you can take to improve things.

The word for "giving up" in Japanese is written with the kanji character 諦, which is also used in the words that mean "understand" or "perceive." So "giving up" can also mean "to see clearly" or "to see the light," and expresses the wisdom of Buddha. In order to perceive clearly, obviously the most important thing is to be able to accurately judge the situation without painful or difficult emotions. You also need to be able to realize that the problem is not within you, but between you and other people. Most of the problems human beings face exist between them and other people. The words "my problem" are like part of a woven fabric. The proof of this is that if you were all alone in the world, you would not be troubled by these problems that arise from your relationships with others.

There are others, and then there is yourself. Stories are created that connect these two parties, and people feel joy, anger, sorrow and pleasure as a result. We become obsessed these stories and constantly ruminate upon them.

These stories, however, are merely one's own memories. Before we get too deeply involved in the painful emotions of our own narratives, we need to see that the solution to our problems is to reconfigure our relationships with others.

When we talk about reconfiguring relationships, it is worthwhile taking a closer look at the underlying connections of power and self-interest and to try to rebalance them.

One way to do this is to give way a little to the other party (remembering that forcing yourself to give too much is counterproductive, since it would upset the balance). Another way is to bring in a new third party (who must fully understand the problem beforehand). Both of these approaches could create new perspectives that might help solve the problem.

The ability to discern between your feelings about a situation and what is actually happening is the major prerequisite for getting out of a situation you currently see as a problem.

It's all right if you can't be who you want to be

Originally, people are passive beings.

It is impossible to live if you are constantly driving yourself to achieve things.

It is easier to live if you are willing to let life go by.

There is a saying, "Be the person you want to be." It implies you can live happily if you become the person you aspire to be instead of the person you are now, that by making an effort you can change yourself into an ideal version of yourself. That is how some people approach their lives.

I believe that this approach is untenable.

As I mentioned earlier, people are nothing more than artifacts defined by their own memories and by the recognition of others. A person doesn't even know exactly what the "self" of the "self they want to be" is.

The idea of "being one's true self" or "being who you are"—the type of phrase we hear so often these days, is also impossible. At first glance, "one's true self" or "being who you are" may seem to be an ideal in which one can live as one's heart desires without any restraints.

But who or what determines that we are "real" and "just as we are"? I am not sure I understand that. In the end, as you strive to become your "true self," "who you are" or "your desired self," you will find yourself wandering around lost in your memories and in the "recognition of others," wondering if you are doing the right thing.

Some people make the appeal, "I don't like who I am and I

want to find my true self," but it is natural to feel uncomfortable with who you are.

We are not born the way we want to be born; we are just born, that's all. What we call the "self" is tailored by others, if you like. There is no way the dimensions will fit from the start, and we may end up pushing ourselves too hard to fit these dimensions. Of course, there are those who still live contentedly regardless. We should simply be happy for those who can live that way. If you can ride the narrative of dreams, hopes and "becoming your ideal self," then there is nothing wrong with that.

But if you feel uncomfortable there, forcing yourself to conform to that ideal way of life will only lead to new suffering.

"I want to live a fulfilling life." "I want to spend my life more meaningfully." I understand the desire of people who say these things. But if you are struggling with these thoughts, you don't have to follow the narrative that talks about living a fulfilling life or a self-actualized life. What I see now is that a lot of people are under extreme strain. They believe they must live a better life and that they must do better than others, and this results in a state of anxiety. There is a desire to get something out of life and to be praised. Therefore, they exert themselves and work hard to improve their work and their leisure. They get anxious if their agendas are not packed full. I'm sure they must be in a lot of pain, and I wish they could relax and live their lives as if the self was no big deal.

But at the same time, I understand that this is difficult.

Humans are designed to exert themselves and are not very good at relaxing. When instructed to relax your shoulders and limbs in zazen seated meditation, few people are able to do so immediately.

But please remember, we are not born motivated and full of energy. If you had decided that you were going to be born, and you had been born proactively, then I can understand why you would put so much effort into living your life. But in fact, people are born in a fundamentally passive state. The proof of this is that babies can never survive without the assistance of others. From the beginning of our lives, we have survived thanks to the presence of others.

If you remember this, you will understand how unnatural it is to live your life in a forceful way, believing that things have to be a certain way.

It is impossible to live actively as if we are driven, when we are passive beings by nature. If you still have to force yourself to live, then you should find ways of forcing yourself that do not push you too hard. But the truth is, there is no need to force yourself. Most things can be passed over.

You might think what I am saying is outrageous. But when you are just about to die, there is not much left. You probably won't even remember the problems you are currently fretting about. When we look back on our lifetimes at the end of our life, we will probably be left with some satisfaction and a few regrets. That is the norm. I have presided over the deaths of many people and I truly feel that.

It is just fine to live your life with the feeling that you are throwing it away. If you do so, you can live much more easily. And, you can die in peace too.

Do something for someone else, not for yourself

If we can think about "what we hold dear as we live" and identify what we need to do, we can create tangible joy and pleasure in our daily lives.

When I tell people that they should live their life with the intention of throwing it away, they often ask. with an urgent tone, "What should I do, when you say I should throw it away?"

I'd really like to reply, "Do nothing at all," but people cannot live by doing nothing. Besides, people might say, "You are a totally irresponsible monk," so this is how I answer:

"It's about doing something for someone in particular, not for yourself."

I'm jumping the gun, but here's what I'm trying to say: people cannot live without some sense of meaning in their lives. And the greatest human desire is to be recognized by someone else. So, how do we get recognized by others?

It is by doing what you ought to do. Not what you want to do, but what you believe you should do. To put it simply, think about what you want to cherish in life, and do that. Who do you want to cherish? What do you want to cherish? Think about these two things.

Do what needs to be done for someone or for something, not for yourself. Don't worry if the future changes. Think about what you need to do, at least now. I call this "deciding on one's own theme, and living accordingly."

I am not saying that it is more advantageous to do what needs to be done. That is a completely different story. Let go of your own gains and losses and emotions first. Put aside the feelings of wanting to gain, or wanting things to be easy; look at what is happening to you right now and think about what "should" be done. When thinking about this, wanting to gain, and wanting things to be easy are major obstacles.

One thing I consider as an example is the way of life of a craftsperson. It could be a carpenter, a farmer or gardener, a chef, or even a clerical or technical worker—those people who are recognized as specialists in a particular field, who are highly respected in their work, who have a set of things to do, and give top priority to those things. When this is the situation, there is little pretense or hesitation toward others. It doesn't matter if these people themselves are valued, because their work is valued. They need no further satisfaction or approval. Since being recognized for one's work is being recognized for oneself, this results in the disappearance of an attachment to oneself.

Their only concern is whether they can produce a good product and whether they can do a satisfactory job. Then, they end the day by relaxing with a drink and saying, "I worked hard today." There are tangible joys and pleasures in their daily lives. It's an enviable way to live.

Once you can clearly see your "should," you will not be swayed by your "I want to." You won't have to worry about what other people think of you every time you look at them. Also, if you do something from a place of "should" rather than "want to," there will always be people who will recognize what you do.

But it does not have to be a big deal at all. You must have a conviction in your mind about what you are doing and be able to explain to others why you are doing it.

In other words, whatever you choose to do, that thing you "ought to do" is not a desire, but a value. However, it will be meaningless unless you think seriously about what you can aim for with your meager abilities and limited time. You must begin by understanding that "doing this, and that too" is impossible.

I believe, though, that everything is an illusion. But people need illusions. Deciding which illusion you choose to live with is deciding what you "should" do. And, knowing that "should" is an illusion, we must take the stance that it is inevitable that things will not turn out the way we want—in other words, we should not expect results or ask for rewards. To be prepared to do that is to live. If you know that the "ought" you have chosen is in fact an illusion, then there is no need to be so hard on yourself. You are a "self" that just happened to be born. To live with the thought "if I waste my life, it's okay" is just about right.

Besides living and dying, nothing else is a big deal

The more serious the problem, the calmer you should be. You have to determine whether you can handle the problem yourself, whether you need someone else's help, or whether you can just work through it. This is how a problem becomes manageable.

After completing my three years of training at Eiheiji Temple, I remained at the temple and assumed the position of *yakuryo*, teaching trainee monks and performing other assigned duties. The following story is from those yakuryo days.

One day, I was reading a book in my room when I heard a voice calling out to me urgently: "Minami-san! Minami-san!"

It was the voice of a young trainee monk. The voice came gradually closer and then the young monk came running into the room.

"Minami-san" he said, breathlessly. "It's something really important!"

I put the book down and said sharply to him, "Nothing is really important except to live or to die!"

"Yes, you are right," he replied. Now that he had come to his senses, I asked him what he wanted. He told me that a certain senior monk needed me and wanted me to come as soon as possible.

But when I telephoned the senior monk, it wasn't anything urgent. The message seemed to be more like, "Please contact me as soon as possible."

The young trainee monk was abashed when he realized the

problem wasn't so urgent after all, but the senior monk was in a department not usually associated with my duties, and one with a high position. Also, at that time, I had a reputation for being very strict, so it was completely understandable that he was in a hurry to tell me.

In situations such as these, a person's perspective becomes very narrow. For example, if a four-inch (ten-centimeter) diameter ball were placed on a four-inch-square piece of paper, the ball would appear overflowingly large. When you are panicking about something, you are in that state. However, if the same ball is placed on a three-foot (one-meter)-square piece of paper, its presence changes completely. You are sure to see it as a small ball.

The same is true when problems arise in life. To use the example of the ball again, if a four-inch ball is placed in front of you when your field of vision is only four inches square, your entire field of vision will be blocked. But with a spacious field of view, you will not be bothered by a ball of any size there. Life or death is all that matters. This is an extreme way of putting things.

By expanding the frame through which you view things, problems that at first seem large become much smaller. Then, you can be calm. How big is the problem really after, once you have calmed down? Is it beyond your control or can you handle it? Do you need someone's help or can you just work through it? That's what you will be able to perceive. That is what "making a problem manageable" means. We all have serious problems that we struggle with.

I understand that those who come to me for advice are often suffering from things that they find difficult in their life, whether they are overwhelmed at work or having problems with their relationships. But to repeat that extreme point of view, there is nothing more important than the question of whether to live or whether to die. Other than that, the decisions you can make are all trivial. If we can develop that perspective, that can sometimes save us.

The only things you can judge for yourself are the little things

Big decisions always involve the people around you.

Your own decisions and judgments are not very helpful.

It is wise not to rely too much on one's own senses or to be too confident.

Situations in which major decisions have to be made are usually negative.

For example, you don't hesitate if the decision relates to something you want, such as to marry the person you love or to get a job at the place of your choice. You don't need to make a decision, you just need to ride the momentum. You just need to say "I choose this."

Let's continue with the example about jobs. When you want to change jobs, and another company scouts you and offers favorable conditions, or if you are in a position to start up your own business, there is no need to hesitate.

But what if it's difficult to find a suitable new job or to strike out on your own, and you hate your current job? In cases like this, people are lost. When you are wondering what to next and you just can't decide, then the problem is negative.

One approach is tell yourself that nothing good will come of whatever decision you go for; you'll go to hell either way. That way, no matter what happens, at least you won't panic.

Besides, major life-changing decisions are rarely made by one's own judgment alone; there are often totally unexpected forces at work. It is a strange thing, a totally unexpected force at work. I myself have been in a situation where the bigger the problem became, the more "compelling forces" came into play and I had no choice but to go down a particular path.

This is how unexpected forces work. For example, when you can't decide whether or not to change jobs, suddenly your boss, who has been the bane of your existence, is transferred to another division of the company. Or a headhunter comes along. Such unexpected events can occur, and the decision to stay or leave the workplace is made for you automatically. If you still have options but are unable to choose, wait it out and don't panic. In time, there will always be forces that will compel us to choose a particular direction. You may end up feeling glad that you didn't force yourself to follow a decision you made by yourself. I've often found myself in a situation where this is the case.

In any case, major decisions inevitably involve the people around you. Your own decisions and judgments are not very helpful. What you can determine on your own are just the trivial matters of life. It is better not to rely too much on your own senses or to be too confident.

If you think you can make any decision on your own, then your perception is fundamentally naive. The existence of the self is only possible within certain conditions. If conditions change, then circumstances change, and a particular decision is no longer valid. So it is a big mistake to think that you can decide and change everything by yourself. That is all you have to remember. Then, when you are in a situation where things are not working, there is no need to be impatient. If you still want to make your own decisions, you should be prepared to accept the consequences, whatever they may be. As I mentioned earlier, you will not have much to regret if you are prepared for nothing good to come of your choices.

You don't have to bloom where you're planted

All things are temporary, established by one condition.

No place or relationship is absolute.

You can choose to be or not to be in a particular place.

When I first came across the popular phrase "bloom where you are planted," I couldn't stop myself from chuckling. I thought to myself that unless I was lucky enough to be planted where I wanted to be planted, what on earth does it mean to be told to just bloom in a place where someone has arbitrarily planted me?

That "place where you are planted" is just that: a place where you simply happened to be planted. But that is taken as an absolute, and moreover, people are expected to bloom there. That is unbelievably harsh. It is even discriminatory, in my opinion, if we are told to accept and endure an unreasonable and difficult position, no matter how unreasonable and difficult it may be, and to strive for self-realization. Again, this may seem argumentative of me, but did Black people have to bloom where they were planted in the United States before the American Civil War, for example?

Having said all that, I can understand why a book which had this title was a big hit in my home country of Japan. If someone tells you to bloom where you are planted, it makes it easier for you to give up if you should happen to find yourself in a difficult position.

In Buddhism, all things are temporary and established by a

single condition. Things in our lives such as relationships, jobs and families are always ambiguous and can only be established under certain conditions.

The Buddhist perspective is to view whatever place or situation you are in now as a temporary one. For example, if you don't have good relationships with your coworkers or supervisors, this can develop into a serious problem. However, by quitting your job, you can sever all relationships with the people in that workplace. Also, no matter what kind of bullying you might be subjected to at school, once you change schools or graduate, then you need no longer have anything to do with your tormentors.

Even a family is a family because its members are physically together. If people are divorced, or if parents and children are separated soon after birth, then they become strangers to each other.

And even if you yourself have chosen the place where you are, it is often unexpectedly or accidentally a difficult place to be. If that turns out to be the case, you can either look for another place, or you can decide to stay there for a while longer. You yourself can choose to be there or not.

The really hard part is when you don't have a choice.

Some people believe that they don't belong anywhere, but not having a place is the usual state of things. Everything is temporary lodging, a temporary place. No situation or relationship is absolute. There is no such thing in this world as a place where you can go and feel safe for the rest of your life. If you decide you want a place of your own, you have no choice but to look for it yourself and to try to make your chosen place as comfortable as possible.

To say, that you must have the guts to try to bloom where

you are right now is simply a mistaken belief that "where you are" and your "self" are absolute. This belief tells us to unconditionally accept someone else's values and to strive to bloom according to those values. This is quite strange from a Buddhist standpoint.

It doesn't matter if you don't bloom where you are planted. It is possible to bloom there of course, but I believe it's enough to simply exist in that place.

Start from a place where you say, "Life has no meaning"

Thinking that you have to do something about a particular situation is just putting yourself in a corner.

When you realize that there are different perspectives from yours, the scenery before you will change completely.

I n Buddhism, we believe that human beings are *mumyo*, a word that is usually used to mean "a state without wisdom" or "a state that is darkened to the truth."

To me, mumyo means not even knowing that human existence itself has no solid basis.

When I say this, people who have studied Buddhism reply, "But it is said that human beings have a 'Buddha nature' just like the Buddha. If we refine that Buddha nature, can't we become as noble as the Buddha?"

Indeed, generally the Buddha nature is spoken of as such. However, the Zen master, Dogen, the founder of the Soto sect of Zen Buddhism, said, "Buddhism is impermanence." This would mean that although the Buddha nature exists, it is neither "essence" nor "substance."

I won't go into detail about this issue in this book, as our focus is elsewhere, but in my opinion, there is no other religion that is as unhelpful and dangerous as Buddhism. After all, in essence it is saying that there is no basis for being who you are. If that is the case, how can you change such a groundless self?

Also, thinking that you have to do something about a situation on your own will only drive you into a corner. It's as though the person who thinks that they have to change themself has a big hole in their chest. That's how serious the problem feels. But no matter how hard they try, they can't fill the hole. If you find yourself in this situation you may decide that the hole will never go away and to live with it as though it is a kind of illness. But when you realize that life itself has no meaning and doesn't need to be understood, you will learn how to endure life while coming to terms with this hole inside of you.

In Buddhist terms, that is the only option. When you realize that there are other ways of looking at the world than just your current point of view, you will feel as if the landscape you have been looking at up until now has completely changed.

This is not limited to Buddhism. It could be any religion or philosophy. Any point of view can be considered if new perspectives can be gained from them. Depending on which perspective you look at it, life can take on a completely different meaning.

The perspective I chose to guide my life in this world was the one preached by the Buddha. I decided that the only way to live with the "hole" I had been aware of since I was three years old and to tackle my problems was to bet on Buddhism; that is why I became a monk.

When I entered Eiheiji Temple to train to be a monk, I fell ill with beriberi (a common affliction for trainee monks) and had to be hospitalized. I'm over six feet (180 cm) tall, and I weighed less than 110 pounds (50 kg). I was paralyzed in my right hand and right leg, and my symptoms had progressed to the point that the doctors told me that I might not return to normal. Despite this, I was eager to return to the temple and resume my training. There was no other way for me, even though everyone seemed to think that I would retire, and when I returned to the temple, I was called a zombie.

I will not know if my choice was the "right" one until I die. But as long as I live, I am determined to bet on it.

99 percent of information
is not necessary

When a person is desperate to do something
about their problems and suffering, they
begin to sort through their emotions.

From there, wisdom is born, and a
worldview for living is nurtured.

When you are looking at your problems, you need to be "educated." When I put it this way, people assume that I am telling them to read and study. But that is not the case.

My definition of education is not the same as simply acquiring information or knowledge. Education is not just something that is nice to have, but an essential part of everyone's life. Why do you need to be educated? It's so that you have a "worldview" when considering a problem.

What kind of place is this world for you? What is the relationship between yourself and this world? Without a worldview, it is impossible to discern these things. And the only way to acquire a worldview is to sort through the information you have and educate yourself.

It is important to understand that "information," "knowledge," "wisdom" and "education" are completely different. Let's get it straight here. First of all, 99 percent of the information in the world today is not necessary. The information you need for yourself is probably 1 percent at most. The extracted 1 percent is called "knowledge." When you can bring that knowledge to bear on your own problems and use it, it becomes "wisdom." So, knowing how to apply the extracted knowledge to your life means you have wisdom. Don't be too quick to assume that with wisdom comes education, and with education comes a worldview. If you don't have a worldview, you cannot extract the 1 percent that is necessary for you from the flood of information that is out there. In other words, "information → knowledge → wisdom → education → worldview" are connected in a loop.

So how can we have a worldview and education? Let's take the example of the craftspeople we discussed on page 38. Many of them, engaged in their own work day in and day out, will not be studying from a vast array of books. But they have their own view of the world. Without it, they would not be able to do work that people recognize.

The reason these craftspeople are able to cultivate their worldview is because they are thinkers. They are people who see the world clearly through their work. So they know what they need and what they don't need. They think seriously about how to do proficient work, they have experience of failure, and they have continued a process of trial and error. Through these processes information is extracted and becomes knowledge, which, through concrete practice becomes wisdom and this wisdom in turn nurtures their education and their worldview.

So, where should you begin? First of all, you must not run away from your problems: let yourself be troubled and worried about them. People begin to learn when they can look at their own problems and issues and really want to do something about them. To get to this point, they must be properly troubled and distressed. When people are desperate to do something about their suffering, they begin to sort through information. Of course, things don't change immediately from there. However, as you repeat the practice of "wanting to use the information" and "wanting to solve the problem," the loop connecting information to worldview gradually begins to spin. It may move at a slow speed. Failure to identify the problem can also sometimes stall the spinning of the loop. But as long as it continues to slowly turn, that rotation should certainly nurture a worldview.

Life is negative, and that's normal

Trying to solve the discomfort of living
with ready-made know-how will not work.

Take the time, effort and patience to
calmly look at the situation you are in and
think about the specifics.

Recently, I hear more and more people saying, "I'm a negative person," or "I lack self-confidence and can't be positive in any way."

Frankly, I sometimes wonder why people say these things. Often, when I talk to people who complain that they are negative, they appear to be leading reasonably stable lives and don't seem to be experiencing any serious problems.

When I ask them specifically what they are negative about and what they lack confidence in, they are not exactly sure. It seems to me that many people are vaguely troubled by the thought that a life not enjoyed is negative.

Some people complain that things haven't been going well lately. When I ask them what's going wrong, they mumble, "Well, I've been thinking about all these things . . . ," but they can't tell me what those many things are. They just have the feeling that they can't go on as they are. It seems to me that people who are struggling can obtain some kind of relief by sticking words like "negative" or "things aren't going well" on themselves, so that they can stop thinking. However, if you are experiencing discomfort in living your daily life, you can't improve your situation without properly considering what the negative things or the things that aren't going well might be.

What is troubling you and what do you need? What situation are you in and how do you want to change it? To determine these things, you need to have the patience to look at a situation calmly and think specifically about it.

These days, we have access to all kinds of information offering advice on how to solve life's problems. But life is complicated. We all have different environments and conditions. If you try to apply ready-made know-how to your life without taking the time to think your situation through properly, there is no way things will work out.

The more you try to do something in the hope of a quick fix, the more likely you are to fail.

Unfortunately, there is no such thing as a one-shot solution to a problem that might have been growing inside you for decades. For example, no one thinks that just one experience of zazen seated meditation will lead to enlightenment. Just as one-time training yields only one-time results, it is natural that seeking instant solutions will only yield modest results.

If you still have a situation that you want to fix, you have to actually try what you think is the right thing to do and apply that solution little by little. Although that can be tedious, it is worth the time, effort and patience. But bear in mind that just because you spend time and effort on a problem, this does not necessarily mean that it will be solved. It is also stressful to keep trying. But still, as you continue, you will come up with a way to manage the problem, soothe your emotions and find the path to what you should do.

You may feel stressed because you are swamped by problems and emotions. Or you may be stressed about putting in the time and effort. Life is about which kind of stress you choose to live with.

If you can hold out until you are satisfied that you have done what you can do, putting aside thoughts of what is advantageous or and disadvantageous, then you have done a good job.

Chapter Two

Shake Off the
Burden of Hopes
and Dreams

People can live without hopes and dreams

When dreams are dashed, people move away from calculating loss and gain and discover what it is that they truly value.

When dreams are dashed, we see things for the first time.

There is a landscape that can only be seen at the end of despair.

I was once invited to speak at a junior high school. The teacher who was moderating introduced me by saying, "He is about to give a talk that will be beneficial to you ..."

"I can't give you that kind of talk," I said, when I stood in front of them. "I am a man of almost sixty years old, so I don't know much about your feelings. I don't know if what I am about to tell you will be of any benefit, but there was a time when I was a junior high school student too. I will talk about those days as I recall them, so it will suffice if you remember only what you thought would be useful to you from my talk."

To paraphrase what I told them, it went something along these lines:

Other adults may tell you to have hopes and dreams. Of course, it is wonderful that those who were able to achieve their hopes and dreams have had amazing lives. I applaud them. But there is one thing I have come to understand during my life, and that is that there are far more times in life when dreams don't come true and things don't work out the way we hoped. In reality, most people's dreams don't come true.

But don't worry. People can live even if their dreams

are dashed. And it's important to learn how to do that. You can look around you for proof of this. Are your teachers and your parents fulfilling their childhood dreams and living their ideal lives? Do you think grandpas and grandmas working in the fields or sitting on park benches need hopes and dreams now? Even if they didn't fulfill their dreams, they are all alive and well enough, aren't they?

So, even if you don't have any dreams or hopes, it's okay. You can rest assured that there's nothing wrong with that.

You may think that I was talking nonsense to junior high school students whose futures were stretching ahead of them. But they were clearly interested in what I had to say. In other words, it was real for them.

I am not saying that having hopes and dreams is necessarily bad. I am just saying that it is not important at all if you don't have them.

In modern parlance, one's dream often refers only to one's occupation. For most people, their dream is the job they want to have, and they want to achieve self-fulfillment through that job. However, as I mentioned in Chapter 1, the "self" that we aspire to is only a very vague entity. When considering a profession, the most important thing is to be paid for helping others. Work is not about your dreams. When people misunderstand that, they allow their hopes and dreams too much dominance over themselves.

The people I really think are great are not those who live their lives fulfilling their hopes and dreams. They are those who live their lives even when their dreams are dashed. They are those who keep on living stubbornly even when their desire to achieve a certain goal is thwarted.

Of course it's good when your hopes and dreams do come true. For example, athletes who win gold medals at the Olympics can be admired for having been strong enough to face the pressure of the expectations of those around them. In addition to this, they are naturally gifted and mentally strong, and they put in the appropriate effort to make their dreams come true. They achieve results commensurate with their talent and hard work, so in that sense, they merely did what they should.

But does that mean that the athletes who poured their blood, sweat and tears into their training but still could not win a medal are inferior to those who did? Not at all. They worked hard to achieve their dream, but it did not come true. They reached out desperately to grab hold of that dream, but they couldn't reach it. I am amazed at the resilience of people who pick themselves up after such frustration and start walking again. Such experiences will surely be an asset to those people as they broaden and strengthen their way of thinking.

I believe that setbacks are important for us as human beings. Because that is when we can leave the loss-and-gain mentality behind.

"I want to fulfill my own desires."

"I want to get recognition from others."

"I want to do what's good for me."

Usually, people are motivated by these kinds of wishes to gain something. We tend to think, "If I do this, it might work," or "If I do this, it will be beneficial, so let's try it." But when you stumble in life, such calculations are blown away. When things don't go the way you want or when dreams are dashed, you will leave loss and gain behind, and look at what you truly value. After figuring that out, you start walking, even if you are not sure if your efforts will pay off. A person who has gone through all this is equipped with a certain magnificence. So don't be discouraged if your hopes and dreams don't come true.

Indeed, our hopes and dreams may become obstacles in our lives. Hopes and dreams are actually like drugs. The only reason we hold on to unfulfilled dreams forever is because we are afraid of the withdrawal symptoms when the drug of dreams wears off. If the truth is that you are tired of having hopes and dreams, will you continue to hold on to them or will you let them go? Take a thorough look at the true intentions behind your dreams.

Take a detached view of your dream and of yourself, the dreamer

Can you really make your dreams come true?

Are you prepared to take the risks and make the sacrifices to do so?

If you don't look clearly at all the things that may not work as you pursue your dream, the dream will remain just a dream.

Even if you can empathize with the point of view I put forward in the previous section, there still may be hopes and dreams that you want to fulfill. If that is the case, then you should have "cold hopes" and "cold dreams." Spending time on fluffy fantasies called dreams is, to be blunt, a waste of time. If you really want to fulfill a particular desire, you have to take a cold look at what your hopes and dreams really mean.

To state it simply, being "cold" means being able to measure for yourself exactly how far away you are from the goals that you have. If you can determine the distance between yourself now and your dream, you can consider the means of getting there.

Is it really possible to achieve that dream? Are you willing to take risks and make sacrifices for it? You need to be able to see things clearly.

Without a concrete image of the path to get to the place where you want to be, there is no way forward. There is no point in vaguely dreaming of becoming XYZ. If you really want to make your dream come true, you should turn it into a "goal." If your dream is a job you want to have, then all you have to do is rigorously measure your abilities, read up on the specifics of the path to employment in that field, and position yourself to grab the chance. And if you can successfully find that job, that's great; if you can't, then it is important not to misjudge the timing of abandoning the dream.

In other words, a "goal" is a "dream" that incorporates the possibility of abandoning it. In short, you need to think ahead and look coldly at a goal, and to be prepared for the possibility that it may not work. To look coldly is not the same as looking coolly. There is still wiggle room when you look coolly at something.

You must be thoroughly cold toward yourself. Look at your dream, as well as the self that pursues that dream, at absolute zero degrees. Purposefully start by thinking, "Maybe I don't have the talent," or "Maybe my dream won't come true." If you do that, you will not be committing to a cheap fantasy.

"I want, I want, I want," indicates strong insecurities

No matter how hard you chase after what you want, if you don't know the reason why, your heart will not be satisfied.

You have to properly identify what is making you think this way.

S ome people want, want, want time, status or money, approval or praise, or a particular situation. They always feel that something is missing. But it's not always the case that they actually want something. There can be strong anxiety at the bottom of the "want." So, when I ask people why they want this particular something, I often get only vague answers. But, when we get to the essence of what they are saying, it is sometimes the case that the "want" is something that is easily obtainable.

A woman who once came to me for advice on her problems said, "In the end, all I want is a peaceful everyday life."

When I asked her what that everyday life would look like, she started talking about how she envisioned waking up at seven in the morning, then having a leisurely cup of tea and a proper breakfast. To me that seemed like something easy she could do right away, so I asked her for more information.

"So what time are you getting up now?"

"I can never wake up before eight, so I'm always in a rush."

"Then why don't you go to bed early and get up at seven and then you can have the peaceful start you want?"

"No, I go to bed late because I'm always so busy at work, so I need to sleep longer in the mornings."

"Then why don't you finish work early?"

"I'm paid by the hour so if I shorten my working time by an hour every day, I'd get less money every month . . ."

And so began the calculations.

If you know what you cherish, there's no need to ask others for advice. If you really want to have a slow, peaceful and quiet morning, you would accept some loss of income. If you want money, you work hard, deciding that rushed days can't be helped. All you have to do is choose one or the other. There is no need to worry at all. In the end, you become confused and anxious because you do not know exactly what you want or what you value. And you mistakenly think that if you can get "something" you will be happy.

On the other hand, some people's dreams are unrealistic. Some might say that they want to live in a mansion or they want to be famous, when they clearly know in their hearts that it is impossible from the outset.

The common denominator with such people is that they feel there is "something" that is not being fulfilled and they are continually in a state of extreme anxiety—without even being aware of it.

"It wasn't supposed to be like this."

"I wonder if I can keep this up."

These are the kind of thoughts that may run through their heads, and the substitute for such vague anxiety is "wanting," or, more specifically, the desire to make their life the way they wish it to be.

I feel there's a connection between wanting things and wanting to get rid of things, a trend that has been gaining popularity in recent years. Lately, attention has been focused on a lifestyle where one lives in a bleak room with little or no furniture, let alone other possessions. But in essence, such an overly simple room is no different from a garbage dump full of trash. What lies at the root of the extreme simplicity of this lifestyle is the desire to do as one pleases with one's possessions. The act of throwing things away is the same as the desire to own things, and throwing things away is simply part of wanting your situation to be as you wish.

You are free to live any way you want. However, you should be prepared for the fact that things rarely turn out the way you want them to. But most importantly, why do you "want" a particular thing? Or "want to get rid of" a particular thing? If you don't know why, no matter how many "wants" you chase after, or how much you try to live in a bleak room with no possessions, the problem will never be solved.

That's why we have to change the parameters of the story. What exactly are you worried about? What situation is making you uneasy? You have to take the time and effort to properly consider and discern this.

There is no need to create something worth living for or something worth doing

If you are dissatisfied with or anxious about your current situation, this can make you want to search for something worth living for.

But if you face the problem and adjust the glitches, there will be no need to carry out such a search.

I believe that just as there is no need for hopes and dreams, there is no need either for what the Japanese call *ikigai,* "something worth living for," or for *yarigai,* "something worth doing."

Some people say, "I must have been born for a reason, so I want to lead a meaningful life," but there is no "reason": you just happened to be born into this world. Of course, that doesn't mean we can't find moments of meaning or reward in our everyday lives, and when we do, those moments should be celebrated.

However, I don't feel that you should worry if you don't feel a sense of purpose in life. You can live well enough without such a thing.

"You say that, but I want to live a fulfilling life while engaging with society."

"I want to feel like I'm helping someone."

"I just feel like I have to find my mission and help people."

To those who might respond to me in this way, I ask specifically who they want to help. They often have difficulty identifying who that "who" might be.

I said to one man, "Well, why don't you do something useful for your wife then?"

To that, he laughed wryly and said, "No, that's not quite what I mean."

I thought to myself, "His wife is a person too. What a strange man he is."

When you want to help others, all you have to do is to think about who you want to help. It's that simple. Realistically speaking, the people you need to take care of will be those who are closely related to you, and those who are close to you, right?

But many people are not thinking specifically about the problem. They are just vaguely thinking that if they do something socially meaningful and lead a life worth living, then their heavy mood should lighten.

When I talk to people who are struggling in this way, I often hear that they are dissatisfied with their current situation and have problems, but are unable to face up to these issues. But often, if they unraveled the problem without emotion, they most likely would find an immediate solution. For example, if you don't have many relationships, make plans to go out and socialize more. If that's not your thing, reevaluate your closest relationships. If you can adjust the things that are not working in your life, you don't have to go out of your way to search for your "life purpose."

If you still insist you need something worthwhile and rewarding to live for, just look at the people strolling around your neighborhood. Do they seem to be living out their dreams and purpose in life? Or does it look like to you that they are thinking that if they don't help someone, they don't deserve to live?

Decide on a theme for your life

Once you have a clear idea of what you value, you can simply let everything else slide.

This makes life simpler and easier.

I once met a middle-aged man who said, "My wife is my reason for living."

For a moment I wondered if he was serious, but it didn't look like he was lying. He worked for a large company and once turned down a transfer offer because his wife didn't want to move. "I've had a few promotions, but I haven't been particularly successful," he said. "Maybe it was because I turned down that offer of a transfer." The man laughed after saying this, and didn't seem too regretful. Perhaps it was natural for him to turn down a transfer for the sake of his wife, and he did not need to weigh some promotion against her. Because he had a clear idea of what he values and a clear theme, he had no hesitation in making decisions about the direction of his life. If he had any doubts, he could make the final decision himself. I think people like this are strong.

What is the "theme" in your life that you want to cherish? It doesn't matter what it is. If you have a theme in mind, it will serve as an unshakable guideline when you are faced with choices in your life, giving you mental strength and toughness.

Some might say that caring so much about another person like that man is a kind of dependence. But even if it is, there is nothing wrong with that in itself. This is just a case of a couple who are close. Taking care of your partner is not going to disrupt your life or cause anyone else any problems. But if "taking care of your partner," becomes a kind of addiction, a pathological element enters the relationship and the two parties enter into a mutually damaging state. But as long as the relationship is harmonious, it doesn't matter how it appears to those around you.

Of course, no one knows what the future holds. Of course you may have a disagreement with someone you consider important in your life, or a time of bereavement will come. When these things happen, you will grieve and feel depressed because you cared so much about that person. But you can't form a relationship with anyone if you are afraid of that. What you do then, is simply deal with matters as they arise.

The more you value the theme you have chosen—or, in other words, the more stakes you accumulate—the greater the shock you will receive when you "lose." But that too is part of everything. Assume that someday the things, people and themes you value may change, or that you may lose them. You should be prepared for that in your dealings with others. To "live the theme" means to bet on what you decide to do, knowing that you may lose. Once you have decided, "I'm betting on this theme," you can let everything else slide. It is sure to free you from hesitation and make your life easier.

Live a life that makes you think,
"Living isn't so bad after all"

Think about others, not about yourself.

Do what you should do, not what you
want to do.

If these are your aims, you should have
more and more days when you feel glad
to be alive.

In Zen, we say, "Every day is a good day." It might be easy to interpret this as "Any day is a good day," but that is not really what is meant. What is being conveyed here is whether it is a good day or a bad day is meaningless. Since every day is a good day, it is only natural that there are no good days or bad days. In short, if every day is a good day, there will no longer be good or bad.

This Zen phrase is preceded by these words: "Before the fifteenth day, it doesn't matter immediately. After the fifteenth day, that's what it is." It means, "Don't question what happens before the fifteenth day, but what about after the fifteenth day?" This "before" and "after" can be interpreted as the first and second halves of life, or it can be taken as asking the question, "Are there times in a person's life that are more valuable than others?"

The old master who asked this question did not wait for his disciple's answer, but answered himself, "Every day is a good day."

For Buddhists, there is no before or after, no good or bad, just days of training. That's probably what he wanted to say.

When you look back on your life, whether it was a good life or a bad life is irrelevant. I think it is enough if, at the time of death, you can look back and say you had a reasonable life or that you had good times and bad times, but you lived anyway. In order to die such a death, we step away from this idea of our "precious self" and open ourself to others. In other words, we need to move away from calculating loss and gain and connect with other people.

It is tedious when you are not much of a person, to have to live until you die. But since you are alive, you have no choice but to do this tedious thing. And the only way to have mastery over yourself is to put in the necessary time and effort on the path you have chosen.

However, I believe that many people are now living in a world of deals and competition, and are exhausted. They are exhausted by the thought that they have to improve themselves, outperform others, and be a useful or great person. But for all people, unidentified death is built in from the beginning. There is no greater task in life than to die. Once you come to that realization, you will see that the deals and competition you are struggling with now are really just one aspect of human existence.

The only thing that determines who you are is your relationship with others.

Think "for others," not "for yourself." That doesn't mean to be at the mercy of others for everything. Work through your problems by sharing them with others. That's what you should do. Do what you should do, not what you want to do. That is what to aim for.

What you do does not have to be perfect. And this is not about being patient and becoming a good person or sacrificing yourself. It is important to move away from the delusion of "my precious self," "my true self" or "living out my dreams" and see yourself as you are in your relationships with others. If you aim for that, you will have more and more days when you think it's not so bad to be alive—or even that you're glad to be alive.

Chapter Three

Don't Be Swayed
by Emotions

Difficult relationships will not change with love or effort

Almost all relationships, whether between family members, colleagues or lovers are governed by dynamics of power and self-interest.

The closer the relationship, the more important it is to remember this.

Do you ever think that your relationships don't work because you don't try hard enough, or that if you treated someone in a more loving way that things would change between you? Or, have you ever been advised that if you want to change another person, first you have to change yourself? But a difficult relationship is not something that can be managed by love or effort. Thinking that effort or love will change the other person, even if it's a family member, will only create new suffering.

Let me tell you the story of a man in his fifties, a man who was convinced he could improve his situation if he just did his best. He worked for the government while caring for his father, who was nearly ninety years old, all by himself. The father was visually impaired and had mild dementia, but he refused any day-care or nursing services, only accepting care from his son. The mother of the family had passed away, and being an only child, the son struggled on all on his own.

But there were limits to what he could do. He lost weight, looked pale and there was even concern at his workplace that he might become ill. The city welfare officer also told him that if this situation continued, he would die before his father. Yet he continued to care for his father, for several reasons. First, he had been brought up by loving parents and he felt indebted to them. Also, he thought that if he did not do what his father wanted, he would regret it. So when his father told him it was his duty to be the carer, he felt he had no choice but to comply.

One day, at the end of his tether, he telephoned me for advice. He was on the brink of falling ill, or wishing that his father didn't exist. Obviously this is something we should not wish for, but in a caregiving situation, people can be pushed to that point. And if they start thinking that they should be more patient or do things better, then they end up in an untenable situation.

I advised the man that he should sign up his father for day-care services. I thought it was paramount that he had free time away from his father, even if it was only for a few hours a day. The man resisted my suggestion, saying that it would be difficult to persuade his father to accept day care and would make him unhappy.

But when I said, "If you die, your father will be even more unhappy," that seemed to convince him. As expected, the father didn't like day care. But I told the man to persevere. For the him, it was a matter of life and death whether or not he could secure a half day for himself. I even told the man I'd talk to his father myself if necessary. If I hadn't been prepared to do that, I would have been in no position to give him this advice.

The more serious and hardworking people are, the more likely they are to assume that if they work hard their efforts will be rewarded. Or if they make some kind of change, then things will get better. But despite anyone's best efforts, relationships are more often than not unrewarding. It's best to think of them that way. It's particularly difficult to try and forcefully settle family problems with compassion and love. The issue of nursing care can be one of the biggest problems when it comes to family relationships. In caregiving, the least powerful member of the family gets the brunt of the work. Furthermore, as the duration of care increases, an inversion phenomenon occurs in which the caregiver becomes weaker than the person who is being cared for.

The assumption that loving care is the norm creates an inverted relationship between the caregiver and the recipient of the care. The dynamic between them becomes fixed; their relationship is closed to outsiders, and the situation between them will not change without a third-party perspective.

Start by stepping away from thinking that a difficult relationship can be managed by your own efforts and love. Whether it is a family member, a romantic partner or a friend, look at the person dispassionately, regardless of age, gender, occupation or feelings. Without training yourself to do this, you will not be able to judge the situation correctly. Looking at things from this standpoint, can you handle that relationship on your own or not? Is there room to change the framework? Or how about severing the relationship? Think about these things calmly.

An important perspective at this point is that the basis of human relationships in any group, from the family to the state, is political. In other words, self-interest and power are the basis of all relationships. Without facing up squarely to that fact, it is impossible to get a correct picture of the situation.

Some people argue against this assertion by insisting that

families are bound together by love. But even among family members, relationships are always tangled up with the politics of power and self-interest. For example, parents appear to pour love on their children. However, in many cases, they are merely making deals: "If you do this, I will love you," or "If you meet my expectations, I will praise you." Also, while they say they are acting in the interest of their children, they are often actually acting in their own interest. Powerless children have no choice but to obey their parents, and the relationship patterns established in childhood can have repercussions when the children become adults.

When thinking about relationships, many people only think about how things are in relation to their own self. And they struggle with memory. If a person's memory is able to accurately capture a relationship with another person then it can provide useful food for thought about a given problem. But if a person cannot see beyond their own feelings and their own point of view and keeps wondering why they are having so many problems, then it can be difficult to find a solution.

You will not find a solution if you only look inside your closed self, ignoring your relationships with others. Or, only self-satisfied solutions will emerge. In this chapter, we will discuss specific ways to stop struggling with your memories, and how to see your problems clearly. These techniques and ideas will help you work with your emotions. This is because often, the reason we fail to see a situation clearly is due to the way we distance ourselves from our emotions.

It doesn't matter if your emotions fluctuate

It is natural for human beings to feel joy, anger, sorrow and pleasure.

Even if you are upset or angry, aim for "steadfastness"—flexibly swaying and quickly returning to normal again.

Since we can't escape the sea of people who surround us, it is impossible not to experience stress and conflict. People may believe that they should control their emotions, but it is natural for emotions to ebb and flow. The important thing is not to get caught up in or swept away by the waves. That is, as long as the emotions do not spill out of the vessel called the heart, it is good.

There is a term for this in Japanese, *fudoshin*, which can be translated as "steadfastness." This, in my opinion, does not mean a heart that stays rock hard no matter what, or a heart that is as quiet as the surface of water that does not ripple at all. It is impossible for a living being to have such a heart. Without joy, anger, sorrow and pleasure, we would be as good as dead. My idea of steadfastness is a heart that can be shaken but will not overflow with emotion. It is a mind whose axis is fixed at one point, even if it wobbles from time to time.

Even when upset by unforeseen circumstances or angered by an unreasonable situation, be ready to sway flexibly and quickly return to normal. In other words, it may be similar to the feeling of walking on a balance beam. As long as you do not deviate from the path you have decided upon, even if you sway or wobble, you will not fall.

The reason why people are at the mercy of their emotions, is because they fundamentally perceive things incorrectly. Nine out of ten emotional problems are a matter of how one thinks about something or sees something. Once you have a clear awareness of what is actually happening in a particular situation, you will not be at the mercy of your emotions, even if they are heightened.

When you are swallowed by a wave of emotions, something inside you is making you misjudge matters. It may be the desire to protect your position, or pride, that misleads your perception. Or perhaps it is because you are obsessed with a particular point of view. To find out if this is the case, all you need to is pause, and employ certain techniques that can shut off the emotion. I will talk about these techniques in the next section.

Of course I, too, have times of emotional turmoil. However, I am not greatly influenced by my emotions. This is because I have mastered the art of keeping my emotional swings within a certain range. If you know the technique of shutting off the flow of emotion once it has begun, it is possible to cultivate a steady mind that will quickly find its equilibrium again, even when shaken.

Learn the art of getting off
the emotional wave

Emotions and thoughts swirling in your head
cannot be stopped by sheer willpower.

There are techniques that you can learn
to keep your emotions under control and
cool yourself down.

When your emotions sometimes fluctuate or get stirred up, there are certain techniques you can learn that will help you keep your emotions under control. I first learned this when I was living at Eiheiji Temple. Eiheiji, the head temple of the Soto sect of Zen Buddhism, is a huge organization with a large number of monks. Even though everyone there is a monk, positions are assigned and there is a clear pecking order. In this sense, it is just like any large corporation. There are times when those in authority are dissatisfied with the work of their subordinates. There are times when subordinates feel their bosses don't understand them. Feelings of anger that are hard to control can arise in these situations.

But we Zen monks have zazen, the practice of seated meditation. Once emotions and thoughts are blocked out through the daily zazen meditation routine, the mind will naturally cool down, and a new perspective on a particular situation can be gained.

"Maybe my subordinate made a mistake because my instructions were not good enough."

"Maybe they didn't try hard enough because from the very start they believed that they would fail."

No matter how angry I was, after zazen, I would often think back to incidents and see how I could move on, and perceive what would happen next.

There is no point in thinking things through if you are caught up in a wave of emotion. The key to developing the "steadfastness" I talked about in the previous section is to develop the habit of being able to turn off a flow of emotion.

However, the emotions and thoughts swirling in your head do not stop when you try to will them to stop. In order to calm the movement of emotions and thoughts and switch the direction of your consciousness, it is necessary to develop certain practical techniques. As a monk, I recommend meditation. It requires a certain amount of guidance and training, so if you are interested, it's probably a good idea to find a teacher.

There are also many other simple and effective ways of shutting off emotional thoughts and feelings, and getting back on an even keel. For example, you can go for a walk, read an old favorite book or take the time to enjoy a cup of tea. Eat a meal alone while savoring every bite, or take a bath while being aware of the sensations on your skin. Doing these things calms the fluctuations in your thoughts and emotions. One woman said that when her heart was in turmoil, she looked at her old photo albums. Perhaps surprisingly, simple labor such as weeding or shoveling snow can also be effective. A physical task that is monotonous or repetitive can also have a soothing effect.

People have told me that a visit to a temple, shrine or other spiritual place can calm them down and help them reset their emotions. It is true that one of the original purposes of visiting such a place is to detach oneself from everyday life. But if you are going to a temple to receive power or other benefits or to be healed, this becomes, in essence, a transaction. Actions that are based on the expectation of something good happening in return will not result in a cool down.

Cooling down is not the same as a change of scenery or refreshing oneself. It is like getting ready to face what needs to be tackled. It is like preparing the playing field for the next game. Therefore, it must be something that can be done on a daily basis without using any stimuli that are new or unfamiliar. A trip to a spa or a vacation may help you to reboot, but this is an example of a new or unfamiliar stimulus—something that is not part of your regular, daily routine. Even within your daily routine, excitement and thrills are not recommended when seeking to cool down. For example if you choose to read an old, favorite book, this should not be a heart-pounding adventure novel or fantasy. It would better to choose a short story or illustrated book that can be read calmly. When cooling down with a walk, a bath, a cup of tea or a meal, you should focus on the senses.

It's important to find a method that works for you—it doesn't have to be one of the ones I just mentioned. But there are two points that you should keep in mind. One is that you should be physically alone. The other that it should be something you can do without moving too much.

Whichever technique you choose cannot be used in an emergency if you haven't been doing it on a regular basis. Also, if you don't do it for a while, it will get rusty. It is a good idea to incorporate the technique into your daily routine as a habit. Like zazen meditation, this also requires a certain amount of training to acquire as a skill. But it is surely worth trying and making it your own.

Don't try to get answers right away

If you put your problem into words that others can understand, you will find a solution.

Try to clarify the root of the problem so that you can organize your response.

I n a difficult or painful situation, just saying vaguely that you're in trouble or that something isn't great will not solve anything. If you just keep complaining that you're not really very happy about something or feeling confused about something, the situation will become messier.

If you can clearly identify what is at the root of a troubling situation, you will be able form the questions that will allow you to solve the problem. This is a key step in finding resolution.

Sometimes people say to me that they've been asking themselves questions about their problems for a long time but still haven't been able to find the answers. But that's because they are just thinking about these problems in their head, allowing their emotions to spin round and round endlessly. This cycle needs to be halted, so that the problem can be properly expressed. Putting an issue into words is a way of turning off your emotions.

Why do we find it so hard to clearly express a situation in words? Perhaps it is because we have not done the work of thinking about our own problems.

When expressing a problem in words, try writing very short, simple sentences that describe the situation and your feelings about it as clearly as possible. Or, instead of writing, you can express the problem verbally to another person, using the same simple language. Then the framework of the problem becomes established. This process is different from looking at or organizing a problem. You are putting your issue into concrete terms that others can understand.

Who is involved, what is happening and what feelings are inside you right now? Put those things into words. Only then can you see whether the problem is within your control or requires the intervention of others. You can decide whether to just let the problem pass, or to actively confront it. You can see how to approach the issue. Organizing a problem into a story that others can understand—before making any decision about who is right and who is wrong—is a useful method for approaching that problem. And that can only be done by putting it into words yourself.

Before you verbalize an issue, working to cool down your emotions is essential. Assumptions you have made and prejudices you hold can heighten your emotions. It is important to recognize this and to try to look at things from a neutral point of view. This is the starting point for assembling the questions swirling around in your mind into a concrete problem.

By switching off your emotions and trying to stand in a neutral space, you will become able to see the nature of the problem and whether the emotion you have been trapped in is hatred, jealousy, anger or sadness.

If you are constructing a building, you can't see what it looks like while you are involved in the construction process. But if you step away from the structure and view it objectively, you can see what kind of building it is. The shape of the building can't be accurately ascertained unless you get some distance from it. Likewise, if you can step away from your emotions to distinguish for example between hatred and jealousy, then you will be on the right track. Eighty percent of the problem will be resolved. Further analyses and decisions can be made later.

If verbalizing a situation is difficult for you, you may want to borrow a "mirror" from someone whose eyes are in their "last extremity" and can see the problem for what it is. "Eyes in their last extremity" is a Buddhist phrase to refer to the perspective of a person who has left behind worldly desires in the face of impending death.

It is when we are at the mercy of our emotions that it is useful to have our situation viewed by "eyes in their last extremity." This will help you realize how absurd it is to live your life saying, "Me, me." A person who is able to look at your problem with this perspective can be a great help.

The most important thing when getting advice from another person is not to be told what the solution is. It is to have your problem made clear. Once the problem is clarified, you will find your own way to approach it, without having to be presented with the answer by the other party.

So don't be impatient to get conclusions or answers. First, you should aim to clarify your problem in your own words, so that you can present it to others. It is possible that you may talk to a person who does not have a clear mirror to reflect the problem back at you. If that's the case, you should try another person.

If you are offended by what the other person says, that's okay too. Just thinking of a reason to argue against them will enable you to move forward. However, if you end the dialogue feeling angry, the dialogue will have been in vain. Why did you become angry? How can you refute what they said? If you are able to think that far, you are likely to eventually find the answer to your problem in your own way. It is important that the mirror reflecting you clearly shows your "face before makeup." Looking at the projected face, how can you cover up or hide the dullness and wrinkles of your skin? Do you have to use a different cosmetic product or can you just keep using the same one? The only way to decide for yourself is to take a close look at your "true face" reflected in the "mirror" of the other party.

Anger solves nothing

You get angry because you believe that you are right.

If you don't want to be at the mercy of anger, take a moment to think calmly about whether what you believe is really right or not.

An old monk once said to me, "Jikisai, I am over ninety years old and thought that I had pretty much let go of most things. I don't want to eat good food anymore and I don't fall in love with women. But, you know, I can't help getting angry—even at my age. I can't distance myself from my anger. The path of the Buddha is far away."

For the record, the old monk wasn't angry about anything personal. He had pioneered various volunteer activities at the temple, such as helping war orphans. His anger was directed at what he said was too much public indifference to social problems and people in dire situations. This anger must have been important to the old monk and must have also been an important source of energy behind the activities he had been involved in.

Personally, I don't believe that that kind of anger needs to be discarded. We just have to make sure that when we have those intense feelings, they don't spill over into other areas of life. In general, however, there is no doubt that anger is one of the more formidable emotions. After all, even a ninety-year-old Zen monk said he could not free himself from it.

"I'd decided I wasn't going to get angry anymore, but I still yell at my subordinates over the smallest things."

"I'm always frustrated because my children don't listen to me, and my anger builds up inside."

I often hear these kinds of concerns.

The reason why we lose our temper is because we have a strange belief that getting angry will somehow fix things. But if you calm down, you will realize that no matter how much you yell at someone, their response will only be to either shrink back or to rebel. There is only one possible benefit to the act of anger and that is to strongly point out a problem. But anger itself does not convince people, nor does it solve the problem.

If someone takes their anger out on you, it is enough to ask yourself what problem that person is pointing out. For example a manager who is angry with a subordinate for not getting to the main point of a report quickly is reacting to the problem that the report is too long and convoluted. Therefore, the person who is scolded should simply give their report in a straightforward manner the next time.

No matter how angry a short-tempered boss may be, you can simply dismiss this anger by thinking, "This person thinks that getting angry will solve the problem."

The reason people get angry in the first place is because they believe that they are right. But being "right" is ambiguous and subject to change. If you can keep that perspective in mind, you may be mildly annoyed for a while, but you're unlikely to become furious.

If you always assume that what you say is right, this way of thinking is as far away from Buddhism as you can get. Buddhism also very much dislikes the act of getting angry. It is even included as one of the "three poisons" (greed, anger and stupidity) that cause suffering and hinder enlightenment.

If you find yourself in a situation where you realize you are angry again, take this as an opportunity to consider whether you really are right.

Most things only exist under certain conditions. If you don't want to be at the mercy of anger, try to keep this thought in your head. And, as a practical solution to calm your immediate anger, it is advisable to physically remove yourself from the person you are angry with. It is also effective to sit directly on the floor (much more effective than sitting on a chair) instead of standing.

Jealousy is just an illusion

Jealousy arises when you feel that others unfairly have what you should have had.

Here are some tips to free yourself from the spell of jealousy.

L ike anger, jealousy is an emotion that also bothers people. If you simply admire or envy certain people for their talents and abilities, there's nothing wrong with that. Jealousy, on the other hand, arises when people mistakenly believe that others have what they were supposed to have. We think others have taken away the situation that we should have been in. It is this illusion that makes us furious.

At the root of jealousy is possessiveness, a sense of being unjustly deprived of something that should belong to us. For example, most businessmen would not be jealous of Steve Jobs or Masayoshi Son. Also, probably no one is jealous of the baseball player Ichiro Suzuki, no matter how much they like the sport. Ordinary people are not in the same league as them, so even if there is admiration, there is no jealousy.

You are jealous when you think your dating partner is directing the love that should be directed toward you toward others, or because one of your colleagues got the promotion you were supposed to get. If you had considered your colleague as a true competitor who had beaten you fair and square, there would be respect there, and this colleague would not be the object of jealousy. You would only think that you need to try harder next time.

Jealousy is the emotion that produces the least positive effect. Admiring someone and wanting to be like them may lead to proactive behavior. Jealousy, however, stops at the feeling of being unjustly deprived and does not lead to positive action. In some ways, it is worse than hatred. While hatred may motivate a person to action, and in some cases may have positive results, jealousy only exhausts a person. Reactions that result from jealousy have no positive effect at all.

When you are consumed by jealousy, you need to realize that this is a symptom of mistaken possessiveness. Otherwise, you will never be free from that emotion. Whenever you are jealous of someone, consider whether the situation is truly unfair. Most of the time, things just happen as they are meant to. You may have thought that you deserved that promotion but the HR department did not think so. You might have thought that someone was romantically interested in you, but actually they were interested in someone else. Even if you think a situation is unfair, it unlikely to be unfair if you look at it dispassionately. It is just that there was an illusion in your own perception.

The only way to be free from jealousy is to understand that. Once you come to this understanding, you can see at once that jealousy is a useless emotion. This is the first step in escaping jealousy's spell.

When anger fills your head, do routine tasks

No matter how much your heart surges with anger, if you separate your head from your body and continue to behave as usual, the raging emotions will eventually wither away.

When anger or jealousy refuse to subside, trying to force them under control is counterproductive. When jealousy and anger swirl in your head, try to imagine separating yourself into two parts: above the neck, and below the neck. From the neck up, or "head," the storm of emotions is left to rage. But the "body," from the neck down, goes about its daily life calmly.

Even if your head is full of anger, get up at the usual time in the morning, get dressed, eat breakfast and go to work just as you did yesterday. Or do household chores. The body will continue to carry out these actions as usual. If you have been invaded by strong emotions, they can stubbornly linger, so you need to be persistent. Stay alert to their presence while carrying out these daily activities. In doing so, stormy emotions will wither away before they become critical.

If you try this method, you might be surprised at how effective it is. I came across it when I was at Eiheiji Temple. At Eiheiji, no matter how emotionally charged the day may be, the daily routine is tightly scheduled from three in the morning until nine in the evening. Zazen seated meditation, sutra reading, *samu* (chores such as cleaning and cooking), meetings and office work must proceed according to schedule from the time the monks get up to the time they go to bed. Even if I was frustrated by the behavior of my superiors or subordinates, my sense of calm would return as I continued to do what I was assigned to do. In this calm state you can look at any problems more objectively.

People cannot change by simply thinking in their heads that they want to change. They can only change if their patterns of behavior change. If you try to control your anger by willpower or self-control alone, you will fail, but if you separate your head from your body and go about your daily life normally, you will appear normal. This is because normal life does not involve confronting people or exploding with emotion. If you work through your anger in this way, you will find that the emotions that have been swirling around in your head are really not that big a deal.

Whenever you are angry or frustrated, try saying out loud what you are thinking, or writing it down on a piece of paper. You will be surprised how quickly you can verbalize the feelings that have been dominating your mind for so long. Consider objectively the words you have used to express what you are feeling. You will realize how much you are thinking about things that don't actually matter to you.

You don't need connections or friends

Essentially, there are only a very limited number of relationships necessary for people to survive.

Too many friends will only create new worries and stress and exhaust your mind.

"No one understands me."

"I just can't figure that person out."

There are people who worry about these things. However, it is natural that people do not understand each other. First, don't expect people to understand you. If you don't know yourself well, how can others know you? Since you can never be anyone other than yourself, you can never know everything about others. If you think you understand someone, or if you feel that someone understands you, that is simply a misunderstanding.

The actual meaning of the word "understanding" is "an agreed misunderstanding."

If we think we understand each other, then we have just agreed to a misunderstanding. In truth, both parties are merely interpreting each other for their own convenience.

If you think the more friends you have and the wider your network of contacts the more fun you will have every day, then of course you should enjoy that life. But if you are bothered by interpersonal relationships, you don't need friends, let alone contacts. In fact, it is better not to try to make friends.

Think about it. How many people are truly important to you, people you cherish? At most, it is probably no more than ten or twenty people. You may think that you have a lot of friends, in addition to the relationships you have with work colleagues. But if your situation changes, those friendships and relationships will also undergo change. When you think about it, there are not many relationships that determine how you live and your way of being. Essentially, there are in this world a very limited number of relationships that people need in order to survive.

This may sound like an extreme opinion, but there is a reason I say that friends are not needed. When you make a friendship, you inevitably strive to maintain a good relationship with the other person. They also want to be understood, appreciated and recognized by you. But that is merely a type of greed. It's good if we receive the things we desire to receive from another person, but this doesn't always happen, and miscommunication leads to new worries and stress.

Having too many friends can actually be exhausting and detrimental to one's mental health. This is because so many relationships must be maintained. And there is certainly no need for the friends we connect with through social media. Why do we want to make so many friends when everyone is tired of interpersonal relationships in the first place? I can only wonder.

If you are not trying to make friends, but simply doing what you think you should be doing, and if that thing you are doing happens to be what you really should be doing, you will always attract people. People with similar interests will sniff you out, and relationships will naturally form between you. With such people, even if you meet only once a year, there will be a deep connection between you. It's almost as though you can read each other's thoughts. It is that kind of relationship.

I have had several such people in my life, and losing them would be more painful than losing a parent.

Once you decide what you value, the rest is easy. You just have to think about arranging your life to include the relationships that are really necessary for you.

People can be saved just by talking about their true feelings

Sometimes having someone else to talk to about your situation can instantly broaden your perspective.

A person with whom you can talk about such things can be a "lifeline of the heart."

Even though, as I said in the previous chapter, mutual "understanding" is an agreed-upon "misunderstanding," people can be saved simply by having someone listen to them. There was an unforgettable experience when I was at Eiheiji Temple that taught me this.

It was one summer day, around five in the afternoon. Someone told me there was a man sitting at the temple gate soaking wet and asked me to go and check on him. I went out and sure enough, there was a young man sitting there, dripping with water.

When asked what happened, he said that he had jumped into the river in front of Eiheiji with the intention of killing himself, but was unable to do so. The river he referred to was just a knee-deep stream. Even though I didn't think he was serious about killing himself, I thought I should stay with him. I took him up to my room, gave him one of my monk's robes to wear and decided to listen to him.

The man, who was thirty-two years old, had been a recluse since he was in junior high school. He says that he went to see a clinical psychologist and a psychiatrist, but the problem persisted and somehow he ended up here at Eiheiji, convinced that he had no choice but to die. When I asked him what caused him to become a recluse, he said that in the fourth and fifth grade he was severely bullied. This is a common story, but it is a serious one for the individual concerned.

I thought the best thing to do would be just to listen to him, so I asked him to tell me whatever him wanted.

But when he started to talk, I was surprised. Although the bullying had happened more than twenty years ago, he hadn't been able to move past it. His memories were vivid, not just of each day, but of each hour, as he started to recount the events of that time.

Initially I estimated that what he had to say would take two hours at most. However, after two hours, the second day of bullying had not yet ended. This was going to take a long time. It was now early evening and I knew I had no choice but to listen to him until he had got everything off his chest.

At Eiheiji, all the lights were turned off at nine. We had to be asleep by ten at the latest. I told my supervisor what was going on, got permission and kept listening.

Eventually early morning meditation and sutra reading began. A fellow monk, who was aware of the situation, brought tea. The man hadn't been to the bathroom nor had he had anything to eat or drink until then. He kept on talking urgently and I continued to listen.

As dawn broke he finally started getting tired. When I asked him if he had anything else to tell me, he hesitated for a moment and then said that he didn't. The clock said five.

When I asked if he'd ever told these things to anyone before, he told me that this was the first time he'd ever spoken about them to another person. At the medical facility he attended, the consultation time was set for one hour, and at each consultation, he had to start the conversation all over again.

Surprisingly, from his childhood until now, there had been no one willing to listen to him pour his heart out.

"I understand your story," I said to him. "Anyway, go home today. You can die anytime you want. When you get home, if you still want to die, call me. I don't mean to put it this way, but I spent twelve hours with you, so I think you owe me that much."

"I understand," he said.

"Promise me this much. Be sure to come back before you die," I said to him, and saw him off.

About a month later, I received a letter from the man.

"Thank you very much for what you did for me," he wrote. "I am now participating in volunteer activities to support children like me who have stopped going to school because of bullying."

I was very relieved to hear this.

It really is possible to move on from trauma simply by finding someone who can take the time to listen to what happened to you. The listener should be prepared to listen for as long as necessary. After my own experience with this man, I am always willing now to listen to someone who needs to talk.

Having someone listen to your situation, expressed in your own words, can often help to broaden your perspective. This is because by putting vague worries and anxieties into words that another person can understand, you automatically organize your mind. Someone with whom you can talk to in this way can be a lifeline.

Show daily care and concern for your family

Stress in the family is a critical issue.

Just as you water and fertilize plants to nurture them, you need to nurture other members of your family with daily greetings and conversation.

Human relationships cannot be nurtured without a lot of hands-on work and time.

Everyone takes a certain amount of time and effort when it comes to other people. That is not always the case when it comes to one's family. Many people think they don't have to take the time to make daily conversation with their own family members. If you don't exchange many words with family members during the course of a day, you must at least display an attitude that makes other members of your family feel that you care for them. Otherwise, it is just laziness on your part. Beautiful flowers will not bloom without watering, fertilizing and tending to them. In the same way, families need daily care and attention. The basic way to show your appreciation is to thank and greet your family members properly. Nothing special is required. Say "good morning" and "good night." When you have a meal cooked for you, say "thank you" or "thanks for the delicious meal." These things should be a matter of course.

For me, this was the normal way of behaving in my childhood home, particularly between my father and mother. It was only after I got married that I realized this wasn't widespread behavior. According to my wife's friends, many husbands of my generation take it for granted that their wives cook all their meals for them. I was shocked. Saying thank you to someone costs nothing. If it makes the family better, say it as much as you can.

However, even I was perplexed at the beginning of my marriage. My wife would get angry and frustrated at me for something that I didn't think was worth getting upset about, and I would panic and think that we had a big problem. But after a couple of hours, her anger would dissipate, and she would ask me what I wanted for dinner as if nothing had happened. I couldn't understand these apparent mood swings.

I asked one of my seniors if my wife was unusual, and he replied, "It's the same at my house. Even if my wife is really angry with me, she forgets about it after a few hours."

I realized that married couples were the same everywhere; that it is normal to get angry with each other but that these storms pass. If we can be quiet and listen to each other, and remember to say "thank you" on a regular basis, these things can help.

So now, when my wife scolds me—the person who was so feared at Eiheiji Temple that my nickname was Darth Vader—I listen to what she has to say without arguing back. I have no problem doing this for the smooth running of the family. With practice, even if you annoyed about something for a while, you can circle the emotion and just toss it away.

The reason why I am able to do so is because I am determined not to stray from the two main themes that I have chosen to focus on in my life: "What am I?" and "What is death?" Of course family is important. But when it comes to anything that does not relate directly to the abovementioned two questions, it's just a matter of finding a compromise. That senior monk I talked to has been able to weather the storms in his home for forty years because he gives priority to certain Buddhist beliefs that he has based his life around.

All of that said, talking back to your partner in a marital quarrel is the most foolish thing you can do as of course this only adds fuel to the fire. To end a marital quarrel quickly, I believe it's the man who should shut up. One reason is that men's logic is often one-dimensional and simple, and their memories of the past are fuzzy, so there is no way they can match women's diverse logic that mobilizes detailed memories.

Another reason is that in many cases, particularly in my generation in Japan, the bigger burden for looking after the home is placed on the woman. Men may not always take into consideration that if we compare unpaid housework and childcare with paid work in the workplace, perhaps house-work and childcare are more onerous in terms of workload and difficulty. If the value of childcare and housework done by the woman is not fairly acknowledged, especially if both partners have jobs outside the home, then women will suffer more stress than men. If women are forced to endure a situa-tion where they feel unable to express their feelings about the sharing of domestic tasks, the probability of the relationship's failure increases. If circumstances do not allow for the sharing of housework and child rearing, the man (or rather, the one who does not do these things) has no choice but to quietly give way as much as he can.

If there is stress in the home, it becomes a critical issue for the person affected. Even if the person appears to be in good health on the surface, deep problems will be developing on the inside. And by the time the problem surfaces, it is often too late to do anything about it.

Putting time and effort into family relationships means communicating without cutting corners. Just as we water and fertilize flowers every day to nurture them, we need to carefully nurture our family relationships on a daily basis. I am repeating myself, but you must keep this in mind. Communication cannot be improved without practice, and this can be difficult if you are not used to it. Start by making sure you greet other family members properly ever day. Remember to say "thank you" and "I'm sorry." That is enough. You can also try doing something yourself before asking another family member to do it for you. Take the time to praise, advise or guide family members as needed.

Still, if these adjustments don't work, you can think about simply letting things pass. And if you find yourself dealing with a load you can't handle, you may choose in the end to distance yourself from other members of your family.

What or who do you want to prioritize or cherish in your life? If you know that, you will be able to find a way to deal with any issues that arise.

Create a "light" relationship with someone you can talk to about your problems

Find someone you can talk to honestly about what's on your mind.

By talking to someone who is like a mirror that can illuminate your own image, you can see a problem clearly and take the first step toward a solution.

I believe that if you cannot see the way to reach a solution to a particular problem on your own, you can always get help from someone else. It is necessary for your mental health to have a person in your life with whom you can verbalize your problems and with whom you can speak your mind straightforwardly on a regular basis. People with whom you already have a close relationship, such as friends and family, are not suitable. The conversation could end up going round in circles with only a sympathetic "Yes, it must be tough." In addition, people you are close to are not always willing to listen with an unbiased perspective because of the stakes involved for themselves.

So the person you choose should be someone you can open up to, but don't see on a daily basis. You should have a compatibility with this person, a moderate distance, and you should trust them. I call this a "light" relationship. Even if you don't see each other often, this person should be someone who listens kindly and accepts your point of view with respect. It is important to choose someone who does not impose their opinions on you. This person should preferably be someone older, such as a teacher or club coach you trusted in school, a relative with whom you have always sensed an affinity, or a trusted boss or senior colleague from a previous job. Look around and I am sure you will think of someone.

As you get older and have more responsibilities at work or have a family, it's likely that problems will occur. It's a good idea to identify someone to have a light relationship with before problems strike. Most people find it annoying to be suddenly ambushed by another person's painful or dark stories. If you contact someone out of the blue after a problem has arisen, they will naturally be wary. So keep this person in your life, even when things are running smoothly, for example by sending seasonal greeting cards or the occasional email. Maybe bring up the occasional small problem with them from time to time. When you need to have a deep conversation with someone, there needs to be mutual trust. A light relationship needs to be developed over long years of communication.

A good listener does not simply remain silent. They should have the language to stimulate your thinking. A good listener is like a mirror, reflecting your own image back at you. When I listen to people, I try to ask questions that will help them understand their situation and highlight problems.

However, even if this person is a trusted advisor, try to regard them as a stranger. It is easier for both parties to meet without excessive expectations and with the feeling that it was nice to talk. If you can see what is happening to you as you talk, you can consider that you have taken the first step in finding the answer to your problem. And if, by chance the conversation sparks an solution, that's great. But keep in mind that you will never know if that solution is the right one until you try it out for yourself.

Get help from a spiritual or religious leader in your community

Spiritual or religious leaders, such as monks, are trained to see the world differently.

Being exposed to the way of life and the words of a spiritual or religious leader may reveal new perspectives on a problem.

I would urge you to include a spiritual or religious leader from your community as one of your "light" relationships, as described in the previous section.

It is likely that you will not find someone you feel you can trust right away, and even if you do, it takes time and effort to build a long-lasting relationship. But if, for example, you fell ill with cancer, you would do your best to find a good doctor. So I'm advising you to do the same thing if you have a mental or emotional problem. Can you solve the problem? Can you find a way of at least coming to terms with the problem and living more easily than you are now? If you have arrived at a critical point in your life, and you can't see a way forward, you have no choice but to find connections who can help you.

In my opinion, a trustworthy spiritual or religious leader has the following characteristics. First, someone who doesn't mind questions, and who does not interrupt your questions or push their own theory. Second, someone who doesn't say "I understand" to everything. Third, someone who doesn't talk about money. Fourth, someone who doesn't brag.

The second is especially important. People who say they understand everything do not give the other person room to think. Such people just want to say, "Follow me."

It is also wise to avoid people who use words such as "enlightenment," "truth," "becoming one with the universe," "living as you are" and other words that are pleasing to the ear but whose meaning is not really clear. Such people are just bringing up abstract concepts to hide what they don't understand.

If someone says "I understand" they are implying that they are convinced about something. When you meet someone who can say, "I understand this much, but I don't know about the rest," then they are at least speaking from their own experience. That person is worthy of your trust. If they say, "I can only tell you so much, but maybe that person can tell you," and then refer you to someone else, then they are top notch.

Such spiritual or religious leaders are very specific in what they say. They do not use abstract words that people do not understand. They are experienced in helping others and can use words that resonate with people. When trying to solve a specific problem, you need to speak to someone who can relate that problem to their own experience and talk about the issue using the right words.

Let's imagine though, for example, that you tell an old monk about your problem and the old monk replies with "Just let the Buddha take care of it." Such words do not actually lead to any concrete solution. But if you feel relieved when you hear that, that's fine. In some cases, you may feel calmer simply being in the presence of a spiritual person like this. It's still an important contact, and one way to come to terms with helplessness and sadness.

Any priest or monk who possesses two of the four characteristics mentioned on the previous page would be worth talking to. It is possible you might find someone who you think is the perfect "light" relationship, but then later become disillusioned with them. But having the right person in your life is really important, so don't give up on the search.

Spiritual leaders such as monks are (supposed to be) people who have been trained to leave secular values behind and are living in daily contact with the tenets of their religion. To be exposed to their way of life and their words can be a stepping stone to change your perspective today and in the years to come.

Chapter Four

Live Life to the Full While Looking Death in the Face

There is a place to heal the sorrows that have overflowed

The time it takes to mourn our loved ones and the manner in which we do it differs from person to person.

Sacred places like Osorezan (Mount Osore) accept and embrace feelings for the dead in a way that is different from more conventional rituals.

Osorezan (Mount Osore) is one of the most sacred places in Japan, located on the Shimokita Peninsula in the northern part of Aomori Prefecture, and I serve as acting chief priest at the temple there. Many people in Japan consider this place eerie, with its *itako* blind female spiritual mediums and memorial services for the dead. Before I came to this 1,200-year-old sacred site, I only had a superficial knowledge about it.

When I first visited Osorezan during the time I was living at Eiheiji Temple, I was amazed at its remoteness and the peculiarity of the topography. In the distance, sulfur spewed from the rocky terrain covered in large and small boulders, and the ground at my feet was scattered with toy windmills and sweets left as memorial offerings.

This place truly feels as though it is at the ends of the earth. But visitors here often experience an unexpected sense of nostalgia or calm.

One day, I was walking in the temple grounds there when I was approached by an old lady, who asked me, "Why would anyone want to come this far to mourn their dead?"

I think that it's because Osorezan is like a large vessel. Osorezan has no set rituals or etiquette for memorial services for the dead. There is nothing but open sky and all-encompassing nature. Each visitor mourns their dead and leaves their grief behind. They come to tell those who have departed before them that they miss them. A custom has grown up that the bereaved stand on the banks of Lake Usori on the temple grounds and call out to the dead. It's not unusual to see a sight such as a man in his sixties shouting "Mother!" in a loud voice toward the lake.

Individuals should decide themselves when the time period for mourning a loved one should end. In Japan, after the funeral service, people put their hands together at the Buddhist altar and visit the grave. We make offerings to the spirits of the departed from time to time. Rites of mourning are determined by each religious sect, and those of us who are left behind will contain our feelings for the dead within those conventions. But our feelings do not always fit easily into those protocols.

Longing for the dead, regret, sadness . . . When those feelings are still spilling over from the rituals that have been designed to contain our grief, a place like Osorezan can receive those feelings.

One day, a couple in their fifties who were staying at the Osorezan temple lodgings approached me. After the death of their only son in a car accident three years earlier, they both went through a period of severe depression and rarely left the house. The wife recovered more quickly than her husband, and when she asked her husband, who was not doing well, if he would go to Osorezan and have the itako communicate with their son, he agreed.

Apparently their son's accident was on the day of his engagement party. They said that when he walked out the front door to go with his family to the party, he was hit by a speeding truck right in front of their eyes.

"Why did he die . . . ?" the wife said to me. "My husband is very eager to hear from our son through the itako."

As his wife spoke, the husband just sat silently beside her. I must admit, I was slightly concerned. But the next day, the couple stopped by before leaving and they told me that they had heard "gratifying words" from the itako. Although they did not talk about any of the details, I was relieved to see that the husband's face had clearly changed from yesterday and a little brightness had returned.

I don't believe that they heard the reason for their son's death from the mouth of the itako. They still may be very far away from being able to accept it. But it occurred to me that by visiting this place, they were giving themselves an opportunity to start understanding how to come to terms with their loss.

It is when I meet people like this that I think of Osorezan as a place to receive the feelings for the dead that keep overflowing from us, and that we don't know what to do with.

You can just live with regrets

It is normal to have lingering regrets about your relationship with a loved one who has passed away.

If you can live with your regrets without forcing them away, you will one day discover meaning in them.

After the loss of a loved one, there will always be regrets:

"I should have done that for them."

"I didn't do that for them either."

"Why didn't I treat my aging parents more kindly?"

"I think it was a mistake to admit them to that hospital."

People with such regrets and doubts come to see me from time to time.

One day, an acquaintance asked me to meet a woman who had lost her husband to cancer. She still regretted not being able to inform her husband of his cancer until the very end, and she was depressed. "If my husband had known about his illness earlier, he could have done what he wanted to do with the time he had left," she said. "But I just couldn't tell him. I couldn't let him know."

In my opinion, since her husband was no longer with us, there was nothing she could do about this now. But still she blamed herself strongly for not telling her husband about his illness. The only thing I thought I could help her with at this point was her sadness.

I took a chance and asked her, "Wasn't your husband an intelligent man?"

"Yes, he was," she answered.

"Your husband must have known the name of his illness. Because he was a brilliant man, wasn't he? He must have realized that this was not just an ordinary situation, since he was not cured after surgery and was getting sicker day by day. Even if you hadn't said anything, he would have known that his illness was serious." Then I asked her, "Did your husband ever ask you to tell him the name of his illness?"

The woman replied, "No."

"He knew everything. I think your husband must have died knowing all about your feelings of not being able to tell him the name of his illness." When I said this, the woman began to cry as if a dam had broken.

Sometimes when I am talking to someone, the other person suddenly starts crying. But this happened at a coffee shop. I had made the woman sitting opposite me cry and I felt very awkward about it. The woman must have been waiting for this moment when someone would say, "Your husband knew." In such cases, simply having a third party say that you were not wrong can save you.

It is normal to have lingering regrets about a person who has died. If it was a sudden passing, even more so. Even if you have done your best to care for and look after your loved one so you won't have any regrets, there will inevitably be some. There is no need to erase such regrets. I believe we should simply live with them.

Then there will come a time when you will discover meaning in that regret. For example, having gone through this experience means that when someone close to you is facing the end of the life of a family member, you can help them by sharing your own experience with them. If they thank you for this, then you can sincerely understand how your experience has been for the good. The same is true if you can comfort someone who regrets the loss of a close relative by saying to them, "I was the same way."

But whether or not you have such opportunities, regret will always remain. It is impossible to try to deny that. So be prepared, and give some thought about how to handle it. Live with regret and sadness for those who are no longer in this world. I believe that living with this regret is the most reasonable way to deal with it.

After being as sad as you want to be,
there will come a moment when
you can suddenly laugh

No matter what anyone says, there is no
need to endure the sorrow of parting.

It is important to decide to live with
your feelings for the dead, and to find a
manner in which to grieve.

One day, a mother who had lost her young daughter came to visit. She had a question for me: "The people around me say I visit the cemetery too often and try and stop me from doing so. What should I do?" When I asked her how many times a day she went, she said it could be up to four or five times. She was a full-time housewife and it didn't seem to be interfering with her normal life.

"So why can't you visit your daughter's grave as often as you want?" I asked her. "Who cares how many times you go there every day? It would be sadder if you just forgot about your daughter."

"But I was told she wouldn't be able to rest in peace if I kept on visiting her . . ."

When I asked who had told her that, she said, "A relative."

"Does that relative have any experience of being dead?" I asked.

"No, of course not."

"Then how did they know that if someone visited a grave too much, the deceased wouldn't be able to rest in peace?"

When I said this, the mother thought for a moment and then she said, "Can I still visit my daughter's grave as I have been doing?"

"Does that bother anyone?"

The mother shook her head, looking relieved.

Another mother told me that even though several years had passed since she lost her daughter in a sudden accident, she still slept with her daughter's ashes next to her pillow. That mother, too, was troubled by people telling her that she should put her daughter's ashes in a grave as soon as possible because the daughter's soul would not be able to rest in peace otherwise. I said this to her: "You can put her ashes in a grave any time, so don't worry. Your daughter would be much sadder if her mother just forgot about her. You should sleep next to her ashes as long as you like."

No matter how hard we try to suppress our grief, it's hard to ignore the pain we feel at the passing of our loved ones. We should not tell anyone to turn a blind eye to that grief and pain.

If you can't recover from your grief, there is no need to force yourself to recover. No matter what anyone says, you can be sad as long as you want to be sad.

The strange thing is though, no matter how sad you are, you still get hungry. If I ask a person who is unable to recover from the sorrow of bereavement if they are eating and the answer is yes, I am relieved. Even though the heart is in the depths of grief, the flesh-and-blood body has the will to live. Bearing that in mind, cry as much as you want, and you will surely have a moment when you can suddenly laugh. You do not know when that moment will be. But it will come. The grief may never completely vanish. So, make a decision to live with grief, and find your own manner in which to grieve.

Free yourself from the thought,
"Why me?"

Once you truly forgive another person,
you can laugh about even the most painful
experiences.

This is the case even if that person has
passed on before you.

I am not interested in ghosts, nor do I believe in them. At Osorezan, people often excitedly ask me if there are ghosts there, but I have never met a single one. Having said that, I have come to believe that the dead are real. Their strong presence has the power to change the way people think and how they live their lives. This is a way of defining "the dead."

The dead are not what the living want them to be. No matter how hard we try not to think about them, they will not leave our minds, and may continue to exist and influence the living even decades after their death. If you are missing the person who has died, one day you will come to terms with that feeling. But occasionally, whether we have come to terms with our loss or not, the dead can make a big difference in a person's life, and this can be a problem.

One day, an elegant woman in her sixties came to visit me and ask if she could talk. She asked me a lot of questions about things I have written, but I couldn't get to the heart of what was bothering her. Her problem seemed to be something other than Buddhism. As I continued to listen, the woman began talking about her late father. The story went back to her childhood. The woman was born into a distinguished family, but her mother died when she was very young. Her father, who loved her mother deeply, did not remarry, despite the recommendations of others. Instead, he taught his daughter—the woman sitting in front of me now—to do laundry, clean, cook and even sew, so that she could take care of her younger brothers and sisters.

Perhaps he wanted to make his daughter into a replacement wife and mother. She described her father as "impeccable, the best father." As a young girl, she learned to do all the household chores as her beloved father wished. By the time she was in upper elementary school, she was giving instructions to the housekeeper.

She continued to perform the role of housewife, attended the high school and junior college recommended by her father, and entered into an arranged marriage with a partner he chose for her. As a wife and mother, she ran her own household impeccably, and continued to take care of her father as she always had. However, that "best father" suddenly developed dementia. She supported him as best she could as his personality rapidly changed, until he finally passed away. Soon after that, she suffered a sudden hearing loss in one ear.

No matter how you look at it, the problem lay with the father. When I tentatively asked her "What did you come here to ask me today?" the woman became silent and looked down. I asked her again, "Are you looking for your father?" and she suddenly started to cry loudly. A woman in her sixties was wailing like a child in front of me. She may have continued to cry like that for twenty minutes. I couldn't do anything, and just waited for the woman to calm down. Crying, she kept on repeating, "Why me! Why just me!" over and over.

Why was I the only one not allowed to just be a child?

I think that's what she wanted to say. From an early age,

she must have subconsciously believed that the only way she could find her place in the world was through her father's approval. She had affirmation for herself in her relationship with her "best father," but after his collapse and eventual death, she no longer had any way of affirming herself. I believe that this intense stress triggered her sudden hearing loss.

The damage done due to the parent–child relationship during childhood continues to have a significant impact on a person's relationships with others at any age. Your gender or your circumstances don't matter. Even a wealthy man over eighty years old who once consulted with me had problems that stemmed back to his childhood family environment.

There is only one way to repair a strained relationship with the dead. It depends on whether the living can forgive the them. Since the other party is not in this world, the forgiveness can only be unilateral. And the act of forgiveness can be very difficult. It is often the case that you think you've forgiven someone, but you actually haven't.

If you can't "forgive yourself for forgiving the other person," you can't forgive the other person. You must "forgive yourself for forgiving." So how do you know that you have truly forgiven the dead? It's when you are able to laugh about your past and tell others about it.

Those who think they've forgiven but haven't really are still too upset to talk to others about their experiences. But if you have truly forgiven, you will be able to laugh about even the most painful experiences. You want the dead gone, but they are still there. There is no more real presence than this. But you can step away from that presence. This is forgiveness. This is what it takes.

Acknowledging hidden grief can help you accept the death of a loved one

Let out your sad feelings, and talk about how much you miss the person who has passed.

Then the day will come when you will be able to recover from your grief.

No matter how long it takes, the time will come.

Mourning is not just the act of grieving and seeing off the dead. It refers to reconnecting with the dead in a new relationship. And a funeral has the purpose of transforming a "dead body" into the "dead person."

What does that mean? Let's start by talking about the difference between a dead person and a dead body. For example, when there is a plane crash, the news might report that there are 123 dead. These 123 people are not exactly dead. There were 123 corpses. In this case, only the number 123 has any meaning. So when does a corpse become a dead body? It is when it is identified as X's corpse, that is, when the corpse is given a personality. When people hear that 123 people died, they are shocked at this tragic accident, but in a few days they forget about it. But if one of those 123 people was your mother, it would an entirely different story. Now there are 122 corpses plus your mother's dead body.

A corpse and a dead body are entirely different. In front of a corpse, people grieve and mourn. If the corpse is cremated and placed in a grave and disappears from before our eyes, will our emotions be put to rest as well? Not at all. The moment the corpse disappears, it is the "dead person" who rises to the surface. Unlike the living, the dead cannot be seen, cannot be touched and cannot speak even if they want to. This is the point where the dead begin to exist in a strictly separate form from the living.

The important thing to remember here is that not everyone will become a "dead person."

A dead person can only be someone who was important to someone else, such as a parent, a child, a friend or a colleague—a person who had a role in your life while they were alive. In other words, a dead person is someone who gave your life a certain definition. More to the point, only those who have given meaning to your life can become "the dead" for you.

How can you reconnect with this dead person? This is a major issue that will affect the rest of your life. Herein lies the meaning of the act of mourning. As I said earlier, the length of time you choose to spend mourning depends on the relationship between you and the dead person.

When the funeral is over and the dead body has gone, those around you begin to tell you that you mustn't grieve forever and that you must quickly get back on your feet. For those people, the "dead body" has not become the "dead person."

Failure to reconnect with the dead person will cause you to repress your grief and continue to burden yourself. Let me illustrate this by telling you the story of a father and his young daughter.

The family, whom I had known for some time, was very close. Then the mother died of a sudden illness, leaving the father and the six-year-old daughter behind. The two never said a word to each other about the deceased mother.

The father didn't say anything because he felt sorry for his daughter, and the daughter put on a brave face because if she cried, her father would be sad. When the father told me it had been that way for a long time, I advised them that they shouldn't hold back like that.

For both of them, the mother's death feels unfair. But unless they clearly acknowledge the sadness and pain of her death, they can never accept their mother as a "dead person." Nor can they reconnect with her.

It is impossible to maintain forever a situation whether neither of them talk about the mother, because their relationship with her remains, regardless of whether she is alive or dead. In this case, it is better for them not to endure the pain in silence but to let the sadness out and speak of their desire to see her. From there, they can reconnect their relationship with her as a dead person.

Then, one day, they will have a moment when they can laugh. For that day to come, they must not run away from the grief of bereavement. They should not try to convince themselves with easy words that everything is all right as it is. They need to look squarely at the emotions they have locked away, unseal them and let them out. No matter how hard they try to hold back and not think about it, the mother is always there. The more they try not to think about it, the more painful it becomes. If they never completely recover, that's perfectly fine. If they acknowledge their grief, accept death and reconnect with the dead person, they will eventually feel better, even if it takes time. Together with the dead, they will rise up again.

Don't think "Me, me"

If you do not get attached to "what I want to do," but instead do what you think might make someone happy, you can reach the end of your life with the conviction you have done what you needed to do.

An old monk once told me that when he was hospitalized after a serious illness and was sleeping in his hospital bed, he had the thought "I am going to die in this room." An intense emptiness came over him, and he wanted to die right away.

When he said, "I wondered what all those sermons I'd been preaching were all about," I thought that he was an honest man.

Continuing his story, the old monk said he suddenly decided to do zazen seated meditation. Needless to say, for Zen monks, zazen is the foundation of their practice. But he had just had surgery and was in no condition to do zazen. But after his body had had a little more time to recover, he tried it. He said that the emptiness that had dominated his mind "melted away like the snow thawing."

The old monk was deeply moved, but if you think about it, it was not surprising, because with zazen you stop thinking and dismantle your self-consciousness. Then the feeling of the "emptiness of death" will naturally disappear.

Hearing the old monk's experience made me understand how zazen can be used even in the face of death.

Everyone knows, of course, that people will die someday.

However, it is only when you fully realize that you yourself will die too that the truth of this really hits.

I am going to die.

When people realize this clearly, they face their fear of death for the first time. What should be considered at this time is not death itself. Because no matter how much you think about death, you will never understand it. It is your "self" that should be considered. Instead of trying to overcome the fear of death, erase the "scared self." If you have a fear of death, it is better to eliminate your "self that is afraid of death" rather than death itself. That is the Buddhist way of thinking.

You might think, well that's all very well if you're a Zen monk and you know how to do zazen meditation—but how are ordinary human beings like me able to erase themselves?

You don't have to be a Zen monk to do zazen. But it does require a certain amount of training and professional guidance. But there are other ways in which you can accept death. The question is not whether you can overcome death, but to consider whether you can accept it. In order to accept death, you must open yourself up. By that I mean to "no longer regard yourself as precious." And, without regard for loss or gain, you must work for the good of others, not for yourself.

To begin with, once you reach your sixties, you are basically someone who doesn't need to be there anymore. If your children are over eighteen, they are adults who can manage without the help of a parent. If you have retired from your job, you are no longer expected to contribute to the workforce. So you no longer need to place great value on "yourself" and "your life." No one will be in trouble without you. If this is your situation, try taking yourself out of consideration and putting others first.

To "grow old" in this world, in other words, is to become someone who "doesn't have to be around." To sum up coldly, after your children are grown and you have retired from work, who really needs your presence?

Even if you have many things you want to do, you may become a nuisance if you do not think about what kind of impact these things will have on others and what value they will have. Think about whether what you want to do has the support of others. If you want to benefit others you don't need to start up a nonprofit enterprise or join a volunteering organization. Of course you could, but you can do anything that suits you and fits with your capabilities. Walk around picking up trash that you come across. Help someone out in some small way. Do what you think might make people happy, and do what you can do right away. It is enough to feel that you're helping a little.

I know a man who's a good example of this. In addition to my role as acting chief priest at the temple on Osorezan (Mount Osore), I am also the head priest of a temple in Fukui Prefecture. Mr. A, a retiree, is a parishioner of that temple. He's a very dexterous person. He has professional-level skills in making prayer beads and in ikebana flower-arranging, the latter of which he can teach, so he holds free classes at the community center at the request of his neighbors. One day I asked him why he didn't teach at home and charge a monthly fee. He laughed and said, "I do it because I like to do it, and I don't need the money."

Mr. A, who is also good at carpentry, once made a chair for us to use at the temple that he thought would be good for meetings. This chair is called "Mr. A's chair" by everyone and is very much prized.

Mr. A surely feels pleased if he is thanked. But he has no desire to be praised or recognized. Nor do his flower-arranging classes or chair making seem to be an attempt to achieve *ikigai*, the Japanese word for a "sense of purpose" or "reason for being." He just seems to be doing these things lightheartedly. But doing them may be giving him a bounce in his step on a daily basis. It is enough to feel "I am a little useful."

Do not be overawed by the thought of being of help to others. Just do things in a casual way, without overthinking them. As you do these things, gentle and warm human relationships that are unrelated to loss and gain are bound to emerge. Then, as you grow older and your physical strength declines, you can say, "It's time for me to close up store on my life" and withdraw. You may say to yourself with a sense of satisfaction, "I have done what I had to do" and "Well, this is how my life has been."

A person with good relationships can pass away magnificently

If you have good relationships with people, even if you live beyond ninety years of age you can die a peaceful death.

To this end, anyone can start at any time to strengthen the bonds with those around them.

If you want to die an easy death, the first step is to aim for age ninety. I have mourned many people over ninety years old and not one of them died in distress. They do not suffer for a long time and pass away as if they were fading away, surrounded by warm end-of-life care.

One elderly woman died as she was having dinner as usual with her family of three generations who all lived together. The rice bowl Grandmother was holding was empty, so a family member asked if she wanted a refill, but she remained still and did not move. When they asked her again, the teacup fell out of her hand, and they realized she had passed away.

Another elderly woman went to bed early as usual, but woke up around eleven o'clock that night and changed her clothes, saying, "I think that this is the day I will die, so I want to wear clean underwear." She changed, and went back to bed. The family wondered what on earth she was talking about and didn't pay any attention, but when she didn't appear the next morning, they discovered she had passed away under the covers.

Then there was the case of an elderly man, whose son used to come from his nearby home to check on him in the evening. One evening the man said to his son, "I'm going to take a bath, scrub my back." The son thought this was a strange request, but settled down to wash his father's bony back anyway. "Dad," he said, when he'd finished, but there was no reply. When he shook his father's shoulder, he had already passed away.

All of these are enviable passings, to be honest. This is what it means to have fulfilled one's destiny.

One of the common characteristics of these people is that they were physically and mentally strong. Another is that they had good relationships with other people. In my experience, those who are able to pass away like this are supported and cared for by the people around them. They have good relationships in particular with their family, including their spouse and children.

As for physical strength and energy, you either have them or you don't. And no matter how many nutritional supplements you take and hospital visits you make to manage your health, it is hard to live a long life if you are lonely. By the way, being alone is not the same as being lonely. On the contrary, many people are lonely even when they are among many people. The important thing is human relationships. As long as you are alive, you still have the opportunity to strengthen your connection with other people.

However, making good connections is not something that can be done in a single day. Relationships must be nurtured with time and effort. In the end, you will have to open yourself up and make an effort to accept others. The more you get rid of unnecessary self-consciousness, the easier it is to connect with others. The key is not to think "I want praise," "I want to profit" or "I want to make friends." Do not think about any of these things.

You don't have to try to overcome death

There is no need to seek meaning or value for your life—you just happened to be born.

Life is like crossing a river in a boat called "self."

The self is simply a tool you use to cross the river of life.

I believe that the "self" is like a boat that we make temporary use of in order to exist in this world. As long as there are people in this world, they cannot live without this means of transport. That is the boat called the "self." You cannot live without getting on that boat, even if you do not want to.

Many people may think that the boat itself has value. However, a boat is valuable because it can cross a river, not because the boat is valuable in itself. If a tool is no longer useful, you can throw it away. This boat can also be abandoned. If the boat has no intrinsic value, then abandoning it should not cause any regret. So when you have crossed the river and your life comes to an end, there is no need to be afraid or sad. You can quickly and easily get off the boat on the other side of the river without any unresolved feelings. People say, "Life is irreplaceable," but in the end, that's just in your mind.

The greatest task in life is to die. The reason why it is such a big task is because none of us know what "death" is. If we knew what death was, we could do something about it. But we don't know anything about this great task at all, and as long as we are alive, there is no way to know.

When I was a young child suffering from asthma, I really

wanted to know what death was, so I asked every adult that was around me, "What does it mean to die?"

Invariably the answers that came back would be something like, "You will become a star" or "You will go to a flower garden in heaven." I remember my skepticism toward these answers as a child, thinking to myself, "What are they talking about? Is this person an idiot?" I wasn't asking about what happened *after* death. But not one adult could answer my question. I realized then that death is something that no one can comprehend.

The most popular image of death is a journey to another world. The usual story is that there is a border between this world and the next, with a judge-like God at a kind of checkpoint, where those who have done good things are sent to a good place (heaven or paradise) and those who have done bad things are sent to a terrible place (hell). Recently, it has become popular in Japan to talk about becoming "a thousand winds" when you die. But a wind is just a wind whatever way you look at it. "I" can never become the wind. It's just another story about dying and going from here to another place or becoming something different.

Because you are "yourself" from birth, even after your body is gone, your "self" continues somewhere other than here, in another form. Everyone has that illusion. But this is not an interpretation of death; it is just a way of trying to keep yourself from dying.

Buddha had nothing to say about the afterlife. "I don't

know if there is an afterlife. I don't even know what will happen to me," are all the words he left.

At this point, however, one thing is clear. Everything is sure to be meaningless. This is because "meaning" is something that people think about while they are alive. But that thought is unbearable for ordinary people. So humans create stories of moving "somewhere" like to the stars, to an afterlife or of becoming the wind, and so on.

There is no need to worry. We can all die without doing anything special. So you don't have to try to overcome death. Nor is it necessary to seek meaning or value in the ending of a life that just happened to be born.

It's absurd to worry more about the afterlife than this life

No matter how much we think and worry about what happens after death, no one knows what death is.

So just take it easy and simply disappear.

Once, out of curiosity, I went along to an End of Life Fair I'd been invited to. It was full of stalls with names like "Cemetery Information" and "Last Will and Testament Corner," and the venue was as crowded as a festival. What surprised me most was the "Coffin Experience Corner," where there was a display of coffins, that ranged in price from tens of thousands of yen up to several hundred thousand yen, and visitors could actually get into the coffins and try them out. I watched a middle-aged woman peer into a coffin where her husband was lying.

"How is it, dear?"

"Hmm, it's pretty comfortable."

Coffins and their contents are usually cremated in Japan, so it's probably for the best if you're unable to sense comfort or discomfort once you're in one. As I listened to the conversation between this husband and wife, I understood that they had no intention of dying. It was a somewhat surreal scene.

I've heard people say they don't want to be buried with their partners, to be all alone with each other in that gloomy, dark place, even after they're dead. But people who complain in this way believe that their "self" will continue even after their death.

The "end-of-life planning" at this fair is a business that uses care of the deceased as its basis, as if to say, "Since dying is not easy these days, let us help you." But business is something that only relates to living, and has nothing to do with death.

Since everyone is eager to live after death, there is no end to the interest in the afterlife—where exactly we will go and what it will be like there? Will it be hell or will it be paradise? When people are seriously worried about this, I always say, "Don't be anxious. Heaven and hell are similar, wherever you end up. I'm sure you'll understand the language and that someone will be there. It won't be so different from this world. And you haven't done anything outstandingly good or bad in your life, have you? Then you'll be fine. You'll go with 'all the rest.' The relatives who died before you should be there too."

I think that a person like me (if I remain the same person after death) would find paradise too peaceful and I would soon get tired of all the lotus flowers blooming everywhere and all the celestial maidens dancing. I would get used to hell in no time too. If you know that you will never die again, whether you are lying on a bed of needles or submerged in boiling water, the pain of such things will quickly cease to be much different from neuralgia. I am certain of this, because I was nearly paralyzed during my days at Eiheiji Temple due to the rigorous ascetic training I underwent.

Worrying about the afterlife is just a way of passing the time. Since death is unknowable anyway, you can think about it with ease of mind. In the end, all you can do in this life is learn how to live in a way that somehow accepts the death you will never know.

In other words, that is what living is all about.

"Books to Span the East and West"

Tuttle Publishing was founded in 1832 in the small New England town of Rutland, Vermont [USA]. Our core values remain as strong today as they were then—to publish best-in-class books which bring people together one page at a time. In 1948, we established a publishing outpost in Japan—and Tuttle is now a leader in publishing English-language books about the arts, languages and cultures of Asia. The world has become a much smaller place today and Asia's economic and cultural influence has grown. Yet the need for meaningful dialogue and information about this diverse region has never been greater. Over the past seven decades, Tuttle has published thousands of books on subjects ranging from martial arts and paper crafts to language learning and literature—and our talented authors, illustrators, designers and photographers have won many prestigious awards. We welcome you to explore the wealth of information available on Asia at **www.tuttlepublishing.com**.

Published by Tuttle Publishing, an imprint of Periplus Editions (HK) Ltd.

www.tuttlepublishing.com

ZENSO GA OSHIERU KOKORO GA RAKU NI NARU IKIKATA
© 2017 Jikisai Minami. English translation rights arranged with ASCOM inc through Japan UNI Agency, Inc., Tokyo.

English Translation ©2023 Periplus Editions (HK) Ltd. English translation by Makiko Itoh.

Illustrations: p. 21 vvoe; all others Elina Li. All Shutterstock.

Library of Congress Catalog-in- Publication Data in progress

ISBN 978-4-8053-1778-5

26 25 24 23   5 4 3 2 1   2310CM
Printed in China

TUTTLE PUBLISHING® is a registered trademark of Tuttle Publishing, a division of Periplus Editions (HK) Ltd.

Distributed by:

North America, Latin America & Europe
Tuttle Publishing
364 Innovation Drive
North Clarendon
VT 05759 9436, USA
Tel: 1(802) 773 8930
Fax: 1(802) 773 6993
info@tuttlepublishing.com
www.tuttlepublishing.com

Asia Pacific
Berkeley Books Pte Ltd
3 Kallang Sector #04-01,
Singapore 349278
Tel: (65) 6741-2178
Fax: (65) 6741-2179
inquiries@periplus.com.sg
www.tuttlepublishing.com

Japan
Tuttle Publishing
Yaekari Building, 3rd Floor
5-4-12 Osaki Shinagawa-ku
Tokyo 141 0032 Japan
Tel: 81 (3) 5437 0171
Fax: 81 (3) 5437 0755
sales@tuttle.co.jp
www.tuttle.co.jp